A Message To Your Younger Self

What Would You Say?

Created by

Antoinette Pellegrini

Book 2: We Inspire Now Series

First published by We Inspire Now Books 2020

We Inspire Now Books Copyright © 2020

Copyright © 2020 Antoinette Pellegrini

ISBN
Print: 978-0-6487645-0-2
Ebook: 978-0-6487645-1-9

Antoinette Pellegrini has asserted her right under the Copyright, Designs and Patents Act 1988 to be identified as the author of this work. The information in this book is based on each author's experiences and opinions. Each author retains copyright over their individual work.

Antoinette Pellegrini, as publisher through her business, We Inspire Now Books, specifically disclaims responsibility for any adverse consequences, which may result from use of the information contained herein in the works by the other individual authors. Each individual author takes responsibility for their content and for any permissions to use information. Any breaches will be rectified in future editions of the book.

All rights are reserved. No part of this publication may be reproduced, stored in or introduced into a retrieval system, or transmitted in any form, or by any means (electronic, mechanical, photocopying, recording or otherwise) without the prior written permission of the author. Any person who does any unauthorised act in relation to this publication may be liable to criminal prosecution and civil claims for damages. Enquiries should be made through the publisher.

Cover image and design : Antoinette Pellegrini

Layout and typesetting: Antoinette Pellegrini, We Inspire Now Books

We Inspire Now Books
PO BOX 133 Greensborough,
Victoria Australia 3088
www.weinspirenowbooks.com

Dedication

For everyone who needs to heal and feel loved.

The first two books in the *We Inspire Now Anthology Series* were award winning finalists at the International Book Awards at the American Book Fests.

Book 1: *Live Your Truth* (2019)

Book 2: *A Message To Your Younger Self: What Would You Say?* (2021)

Contents

Introduction: The Inspiration	*Antoinette Pellegrini*	1
The Girl In The Mirror	*Antoinette Pellegrini*	9
I Am The Key	*Lisa Locks*	25
Steven Up	*Stefano D'Agata*	39
Somewhere Over The Red Sky	*Christine Carmuciano*	59
Jump In Puddles: Releasing My Inner Child	*Diane Psaila*	79
Dreams Can Come True	*Gail Conley*	101
How $6 Changed My Life	*Suzanne Therese Costello*	117
Breaking Through	*Lisa Jane Hussey*	137
Glimpses Of Me	*Kathy Zisiadis*	155
The Young Girl Who Was Too Scared to Cry	*Anne-Marie Donis*	177
Our Messages		193
Author Bios		209

Introduction

The Inspiration

Antoinette Pellegrini

The first time I met my younger self was over 20 years ago. It was 1999, and I was sitting in a large auditorium in Melbourne for the Metaphysical Mastery event, very excited that I would soon be hearing from Deepak Chopra, James Redfern and Wayne Dyer, authors whom I admired and who had opened my eyes to new and exciting possibilities about spirituality and the nature of reality.

I was eagerly anticipating their entrance, but first Terah Kathyrn Collins entered the stage. I didn't know who she was, but the program said she was an internationally known speaker, feng shui teacher, and neuro-linguistic practitioner.

I know I enjoyed the day, but the only detail I remember is the guided meditation that Terah took us through. She said she was going to take us on a journey to meet our younger selves. I was intrigued. I had never done this before. She asked us to relax, breathe deeply and imagine our younger self standing in front of us.

It worked. I could see myself standing there in front of me. I was about 10-years-old with my hair in pigtails and ribbons, dimples in both cheeks and big wide eyes.

I looked at the little girl in front of me, and although she was smiling, I could see the weight of expectations she already carried. The need to live up to what her parents wanted and expected, and the weight of doing the right thing when all she wanted was love and acceptance, was visible in her eyes. But I also saw in her eyes, promise and excitement for the future. The world was still full of possibilities.

I started crying. Tears were rolling down my face, uncontrollable tears. It took me by surprise. What was I crying about? Who was I crying for? Was it for the pain that this little girl would have to go through? Was it for the promises, the hopes, and dreams that would remain unfulfilled? I wasn't sure. All I knew is that I couldn't stop the tears. In an auditorium full of thousands of people, I felt alone, just me and a little girl that was also me.

The meditation had come to an end, so I had to say goodbye to that little girl. I gave her a big hug. But even after the meditation had ended, I could still see and feel that little girl and I felt so sad. Was it sadness for her then or for me and where I was in my life, or was it for both?

This was a time when I had just begun my quest to find me and what fulfilled me. I didn't want to leave that little girl. I wanted to keep holding her, to tell her that everything would be alright, that above all she was loved. I promised one day that I would come back to her. It has taken me a while, but with this book, my promise to her has been kept.

This book is the second in my *We Inspire Now Series*. I created the anthology series so that everyday people can find a voice and share their inspiring stories with others. These might be stories of overcoming difficulties and challenges, stories about healing themselves and helping others to heal, stories about living their passion and making their lives better and happier.

I was very honoured that the first book in the series, *Live Your Truth*, was a finalist in its category at the 2019 International Book Awards sponsored by the American Book Fest. It was validation that the stories of 10 people from Melbourne could touch the hearts of people on the other side of the world.

We all have inspiring stories to tell. No matter where we come from, the issues we face are universal.

So why choose to write *A Message to Your Younger Self?*

When I first thought about this topic for the second book in the *We Inspire Now Series,* I thought it might be helpful as advice and inspiration for younger people, from the perspective of people who were older and hopefully wiser. There is an element of this in these stories.

However, my experience has shown that books have a way of being much more than the author originally intended. What you think you're writing about is not always what takes shape on the page. Writing sometimes takes on a life of its own and becomes what it probably was always meant to be.

This book and these stories are very personal, and yet in some ways, they are also universal. I hope that they will resonate with you, some more than others no doubt, and will remind you of your own experiences and emotions.

Hindsight is a wonderful thing. Looking back at your life and at all the key decisions and events that shaped you and that took you in a certain direction, what do you say to yourself?

If only you knew then what you know now? Do you wish some things had never happened? Do you wish you had chosen differently? Personally, I would say 'Yes' to those questions concerning some aspects of my life, but at the same time, I know that I can't change the past.

My past events and decisions are what brought me to where I am today. Whilst I can't change the past, I can certainly change how I think about the past.

The past still influences us, but only if we let it. Are you carrying the past with you? Is it still shaping you and influencing your decisions? Are you consciously or unconsciously bringing the past into your present?

All we have is the present, and it's the decisions we make today that are creating our future selves. It's our thoughts, feelings and attitude that are shaping our decisions in the present. And it's these feelings, decisions and choices that we make now that create our future selves. So in talking to your younger self what you are really doing is changing your thinking today.

This is supported by the latest scientific research.

A 2018 study conducted by Robin Kowalski and Annie McCord and published in *The Journal of Social Psychology*[1] asked several hundred people over the age of 30 questions about themselves, including what advice they would give their younger selves. The advice fell into the categories of relationships, money, a sense of self and life goals.

More importantly, the study also asked whether participants started following the advice they wished

---

[1] Kowalski, Robin M. and McCord, Annie, *If I Knew Then What I Know Now: Advice to my Younger Self*, The Journal of Social Psychology, DOI: <u>10.1080/00224545.2019.1609401,</u>
<u>https://www.tandfonline.com/doi/abs/10.1080/00224545.2019.1609401?journalCode=vsoc20&</u>

they could have given themselves. It found that 67 per cent of people had started following their own advice, and it had made a positive difference to their current lives. Kowalski and McCord wrote:

'The results of the current studies suggest that, rather than writing to Dear Abby, we should consult ourselves for advice we would offer to our younger selves. The data indicates that there is much to be learned that can facilitate well-being and bring us more in line with the person that we would like to be should we follow that advice.' [2]

What would you say to your younger self? What advice would you give? What wisdom from hindsight do you have?

In so doing, do not look at your past in judgement about what you did right or wrong, or what you would like to change. Rather, look at it from the perspective of what encouragement would you give your younger self. It is an opportunity to take that encouragement into your life now. Remember, no matter what has happened, you have survived, you are here, you are alive, and being alive always comes with new choices and possibilities.

---

[2] Hendricks, Scotty, https://bigthink.com/personal-growth/advice-to-younger-self?utm_source=All+Big+Think+Newsletters&utm_campaign=084c695c89-EMAIL_CAMPAIGN_2019_04_10_02_29_COPY_01&utm_medium=email&utm_term=0_4d b4d7150a-084c695c89-43546641, 18 June 2019, page 2, reviewing the research by Kowalski and McCord.

The Inspiration

I encourage you to look back at your younger self and imagine what you would say to that little girl or little boy that you were. Just imagine giving them a big hug because sometimes it is what they need more than anything else. Tell your younger self that you are okay, that you will survive, and perhaps the most important message of all, that you are loved. I believe that the most important message to give yourself is that you love and accept who you are.

For above all, *A Message to Your Younger Self* is an opportunity to heal. The co-authors in this book share their personal stories and messages to their younger selves and overwhelmingly, they have all said that it has been a healing experience. There were tears of joy and sadness. Some have healed past wounds, some were able to see their past experiences from a new perspective, and some were able to draw strength from their younger self. You may see yourself mirrored in some of the stories.

The biographies of all the co-authors are at the back of the book. I encourage you to read them. The last chapter of the book also summarises the main messages in each of their stories.

Messages to your younger self touches you even when you least expect it. Recently I saw the movie *Rocketman* about the life of the amazing musician and singer, Elton John. He has touched the lives of millions with his music. What I hadn't realised was that the movie wasn't just about his life but was the story of Elton healing himself by repairing the hurt inside him from when he was young.

A Message To Your Younger Self

One of the last scenes in the movie is Elton hugging his younger self. I cried, as did many others who saw the movie. I cried for the young Elton who hurt so much, I cried for my younger self and remembered when I hugged that little girl and told her she was good enough and she was loved. I cried for so many of our younger selves who are hurting and feeling not good enough and not loved enough and felt the healing for so many of us.

Ultimately, *A Message to Your Younger Self* is really about healing and love. It's healing the past, taking that healing into the present, and loving the person you were and are today.

In this compilation, ten people took the journey to refect and speak with their younger selves. I hope that you enjoy this anthology and that it inspires you to take your own journey to meet your younger self.

What would you say?

The Girl In The Mirror

Antoinette Pellegrini

Be you. Be who you really are.
That is not only enough, it is everything.
Antoinette Pellegrini

A Message To Your Younger Self

It was a Monday night, and I was at a spiritual group I regularly attended. The guided meditation was starting, and we were asked to imagine ourselves on a beach and immerse ourselves in the water, the waves washing away any negative feelings. Instead, I found myself going back in time – back 49 years to when I was 10, and I was drowning.

I had been walking in the ocean with my aunt. We had been walking together, chatting about nothing in particular. I was having fun - going to the beach was a rare occurrence when I was young. It was a beautiful sunny day, the water was cool, and the waves gentle, and I felt comfortable with the water reaching my chest.

Another step, and suddenly the seafloor gave way under my feet. I was under the water. I felt a moment of panic and then a total calm. I could see my face. I have heard that people who have had near-death experiences say that they remember looking down at their dying body. I can't say exactly what happened to me, but I do remember looking at myself.

My eyes were wide open and startled, filled with fear, my hair was floating upwards, and my arms were flaying. My mouth was wide open, with bubbles of air escaping and floating upwards. I was watching my life floating away. Yet I felt calm. I was watching myself as if I were watching a movie. No, it was even more detached than that. I was calmly and unemotionally watching myself die.

The next thing I remember I was sitting on the sand and I could hear my worried aunt saying, 'Please do not tell your mum what just happened.' I answered, 'Okay Zia, I won't tell her.'

It was an easy promise to make as I wasn't sure what had happened. I had been watching myself drown and then suddenly I was on the shore. How did I get back on to the shore? What happened between watching the air bubbles escape from my mouth and sitting on the sand? I don't know. I have no memory of it. However, I did break my promise and told my mother, but it was more than 30 years later, long after my aunt had passed away.

Back in the meditation, I saw this little girl again. This time I held her and realised that it had been a decision point. I had a choice at 10 years of age to leave this Earth. I chose not to. Maybe my spirit knew of the difficulties and hardships ahead of me and was giving me a choice. I am very grateful to my ten-year-old self for having the courage to stay.

My first message to my younger self is: Thank you for choosing life.

The difficulties and challenges had started before I was 10. Being the eldest of four daughters of Italian immigrants, I didn't speak any English when I started school at five years of age. It must have been difficult in those early days of school, being in an unfamiliar environment, not knowing anyone and not knowing how to speak the language. But curiously, I have very few memories of that time.

One incident I remember very clearly is when I was in Grade 1, sitting with my mother and younger sister who had started school that year, reading aloud from a book, and my mother criticising me for not reading well enough. 'You are making mistakes. That's not good enough. Your sister is in Prep, and she reads better than you.'

I was devastated. I hadn't realised that it was a competition. My sister had the advantage of being exposed to the English language before she started school, but regardless, it was a turning point. I knew that to make my mother happy, I had to not only work hard at school, I had to be better than my sisters. I hated that competition. It was the start of my feeling that no matter what I did, I was never going to be good enough.

My parents did their best, and they did love us, but they didn't know how to show love. Their love was expressed through working hard, providing for us and pushing us to do our best, rather than giving us hugs and telling us they loved us.

The competition had started even earlier through piano lessons. My cousin had started playing the piano, so of course, my sister and I had to learn. It was a competition in my father's eyes as well. We had to be better than others, so at five years of age and my sister even younger at four, we both started learning to play the piano.

I didn't enjoy it but what I hated the most was the performances we had to do when relatives came over. I dreaded getting visitors. My sister was better at playing the piano than me. Perhaps she was more naturally gifted or perhaps her heart was in it more. All I felt was that no matter what I did, I wasn't going to be good enough. I thought the relatives hated it too, forced to listen to us and congratulate us on how well we played. Did they also wish it was over?

Playing the piano continued until my early teens when l was old enough to say no more. It was such a relief! No more performances, no more feeling that I wasn't good enough, at least in relation to playing the piano.

What I was to find out much later, in fact, last year at the age of 58, was that one of my younger cousins loved to hear us play the piano. So much so, that it inspired him to take up a career in music, which he is still in today.

Knowing this lifted my spirits and showed me that we don't always know the impact we have on other people's lives. If only I could tell that little girl sitting at the piano hating her performances, that she was impacting someone else's life so positively and instilling in them a love of music. I am sure that she would have felt uplifted knowing she was making such a positive difference to someone. We all make a difference to other people's lives, whether we realise it or not.

Sometimes we know the difference we make, whether it's helping a friend in time of need, being a positive role model to your children and others, or in my case, helping clients to achieve their writing and personal goals. Often, however, we are unaware of the impact we are making, either positive or negative.

I'm reminded of an incident that happened to me before I had children. I was at a pedestrian crossing, and the light had turned green, indicating it was safe to cross. I was about to step onto the road when someone from behind grabbed me and pulled me back. In that moment a car zoomed through the red light. He would have run me over. The man who grabbed me apologised. I was so shaken at that moment that I didn't even see his face, but he saved my life and the life of my children yet to be born.

We often never find out the impact of our actions, the kind words, the smiles we give a stranger as we walk by and the help we give others. It was only 50 years later that I found out about the positive impact my playing piano had on someone else's life. So to that little girl on the piano, your efforts did make a positive difference to at least one person, and that is enough.

In fact, wanting to make a positive difference is, in many ways, what has driven me forward in life. In every workplace, in every interaction with people, in my teaching and my writing, my goal has been to make a positive impact.

We all make a difference in the world. Whether this is a positive or negative difference is very much up to us. I will take this message forward with me and aim to leave the world a better place because I was there.

However, the little girl sitting on the piano didn't understand this yet, and the feeling of not being good enough was to remain for many years to come.

There were fun times as well when I was young. It was a time of simple pleasures. We grew up in Fawkner, in a typical suburban Melbourne block that my father had turned into a small farm, replicating as closely as he could the farm in the small town in Abruzzo, Italy, where he grew up.

Half of the backyard was devoted to growing what seemed to be an enormous assortment of fruit and vegetables in a relatively small space. The other half housed a variety of animals that belonged on a farm and not in a suburban back yard. We had the usual pets: dogs, cats and a budgie, but we also had chickens, rabbits and guinea pigs. At various times, a goat, sheep, ferrets and even a turtle were added to the menagerie.

The animals were a constant source of amusement. I remember one eventful Easter Sunday when the goat escaped. Our house was situated across the road from the local church. Just at the time when people were leaving the church following the Easter service, our goat managed to get out of the usually locked gate and ran down the street. Women and children were screaming. Others were laughing. My dad, sisters and I took chase and eventually recaptured our wayward goat.

My sisters and I loved feeding and playing with the animals. We treated them as pets but were careful not to get too attached to some as invariably our pet chickens, rabbits, sheep and even the goat, eventually become dinner.

Being self-sufficient was important to my parents. Dad was always saying, 'You need to be prepared, in case there is another war.' Looking back, I can understand this. During World War II, the town my parents had come from was the front line between the German and American troops. Mum told us many times how German soldiers had come to their house one night and said, 'Get out! Now!' They had been refugees and were not able to return to their homes until the war had ended.

Determined to make sure we were prepared for war, Dad insisted that my sisters and I learnt to shoot. So our suburban back yard became a target shooting range, although Dad did make sure that our neighbours were not in their backyard at the time. He would put plums on the back fence and with an air-rifle, we had to shoot them. He would yell, 'Aim. Fire!' and he was never satisfied until we were successful at knocking the plums off the fence.

I imagine our upbringing was very different from the typical Australian child.

Growing up, my three sisters and I didn't have many toys and the ones we did have, we had to share. We had one doll between two of us and one bike between the four of us. We must have felt deprived of dolls because we often dressed up some of the animals, including putting a nappy on the turtle! I hope that we didn't cause them too much distress.

We learnt to share and, without other alternatives, we used our imagination. We created epic stories that we played out, with fairies, witches and heroes. We found fun in household appliances and furniture – a blanket thrown over a table became a cubby house; the Hills Hoist clothesline became a merry-go-round, each of us clinging on to a corner and spinning it round and round.

We found joy in making daisy chains and chasing butterflies. We found wonder everywhere. This is something that I hope to take forward with me, inspiration from my younger self to find the wonder and pleasure in the small things all around us.

The weight of expectation, of doing the right thing was, however, never far away.

I did do well at school, and at university, after all, it is what was expected. However, it never seemed to be good enough for my parents, my father in particular. He expected me to achieve and to do better than others, better than my sisters, better than my school friends. I tried my best to meet these expectations, but it wasn't who I was or what I wanted. I just wanted a big hug and to be told that I was loved and good enough just the way I was.

And no matter how hard I tried, it was never enough for my father. Whenever I achieved something significant, my father would boast about it to others - family, friends and relatives - because for him it was what others thought that really mattered.

The issue for me was that he didn't just boast about what I had achieved, he always exaggerated it - B became A, A became A+, best in class became best in the year level. Even when much later I received an award for the best student for Commercial Law at RMIT University, that became the best student in Australia! I was never enough.

I remember a comment Dad made when one day when I was in my thirties. He had spent the whole day complaining I hadn't done things the right way. I was a sole parent at the time, and my boys were still very young. I was only doing my best, but that didn't seem to be good enough. My boys weren't dressed well enough, I looked shabby, the food I made wasn't good enough, and the house wasn't clean enough. I can't even remember everything he had said, but I just snapped and started yelling at him to stop it.

'Stop it! Why are you always criticising me? Why am I never good enough for you?' It was uncharacteristic of me, and he was taken aback. I still remember the surprised look on his face as he explained, 'It's just that I love you so much, and I want you to be perfect.'

I was deflated. Obviously, I wasn't perfect in my Dad's eyes. It was confirmation that I wasn't good enough. I was never going to be good enough for him. What I realise now is that my parents were only doing their best, doing what they thought was right, and Dad thought he was helping and encouraging me. I understand now and forgive him. He had no idea of the negative effect his words were having on me.

So it wasn't very surprising that at 15 I found myself looking in the mirror, hating what I saw.

My father had focused primarily on my academic achievements with his constant mantra, 'You need to study hard, achieve high marks and always do better.' However, my feelings of not being good enough extended much further than this. As I stood and looked at my 15-year-old self in the mirror, I couldn't find anything I liked. I hated how I looked – I wasn't slim enough, I wasn't pretty enough, I wasn't cool enough or trendy enough – I just wasn't enough!

It was later in that year that I was to experience the first time a male showed interest in me. It set up a pattern that would last a very long time.

The Catholic girls' school I attended was having a formal ball with the local Catholic boys' school. The boys visited for rehearsals, and we were all excited and a bit nervous. We were learning progressive dances, and it was fun. A few days later, one of my girlfriends

A Message To Your Younger Self

came up to me to say that one of the boys liked me and wanted to meet me. I couldn't believe it. Me!

He liked me! Who was he? I had no idea. I couldn't believe that he liked me, amongst all of the other girls. I agreed to meet him, and we went for a walk around the park. We met up a few times, and it was all very innocent. We shared a kiss. It was my first kiss and I will always remember it, but our relationship never went beyond this, mainly due to my feelings of insecurity and unworthiness.

About forty years later, I was to catch up with him for a coffee. He was successful and lived overseas with his wife and family. He was back in Melbourne for a short visit and contacted me through LinkedIn, suggesting we catch up. I was excited and more than a little nervous. Forty years is a long time, and I definitely didn't look the same as I did when I was 15. The question, 'What if?' lingered. What if back then I had dared to take things further? This falls into the category of paths untaken, and we never know where the unknown paths might have taken us.

There would be many more crossroads in my life where that question, 'What if I had taken that different path?' sometimes crossed my mind. However, there is no point dwelling on this. I cannot change the past. I can only change how I think about the past.

What this encounter with a boy who liked me did was to start a pattern that was to continue for most of my life – a boy likes me so I must be okay. I didn't feel good enough, but if I man wanted me, then I must be good enough in his eyes.

Looking back at my two failed marriages, and other relationships, was I really just yearning for the love and intimacy I didn't get when I was young? When a man wanted to be with me, and even wanted to marry me, I remember thinking, 'He wants me so I must be good enough for him.' I sought my validation in other people's love, but this never works in the long run.

My first marriage ended when my husband walked out, and I was left with bringing up a two-year-old and a three-month-old baby on my own. To say I was devastated is an understatement, and the difficulties of bringing up two young children as a sole parent were compounded by my feelings of unworthiness. Why had he left? It wasn't for another woman. Perhaps I just wasn't good enough.

A few years later, I met the man who would be my second husband. Our marriage lasted three years, but even before we were married, the universe, my gut, my intuition was screaming at me that this was not right. I knew that he wasn't right for me, that it wasn't going to work, but I ignored it. The need for love and validation overrode my intuition.

One vivid example of this was when we were looking for an engagement ring. I was adamant that I wanted the ring to be different from my first engagement ring. We had looked in what seemed to be every jewellery store in Melbourne. Finally, I found a ring that I loved. I was thrilled with it until I got home.

I wanted to compare the rings, so I got my old engagement ring out. I put them side by side and just stared in disbelief. I had been determined that I wanted something totally different, yet the rings were identical except that my new one was bigger! It had the same intricate crossover design and the same diamond cut.

I knew immediately that this was a message, a sign that this was not the right marriage for me, but I again ignored it.

My intuition and inner voice were right; the universe was right; my gut was right. I just needed to listen and follow it. But I didn't. After all, he loved me.

So I ignored the fact that our interests, and more importantly, our values were so different. He was into war games and mediaeval role-playing, and I was discovering spirituality and learning Reiki, a hands-on healing modality.

I remember an incident which shone a light, like a beacon, on to our differences. One Sunday afternoon he came to me very excited and proud of himself. 'I've created a website for us, come and have a look.' I followed him into the study and on the front page of the website in huge letters was 'Contact us for War Games and Reiki.' I stared in disbelief. 'You can't have those two things together. Please take me and Reiki out of it.' He was devastated and hurt, and although I tried to explain it to him, he didn't understand why I was upset. He didn't understand that those two things were diametrically opposed, and so were we. It was inevitable that the marriage would end.

This pattern of seeking external validation and love from a man continued, but it was a flawed assumption and always doomed to fail. Another person, another man, cannot complete you. We talk about our 'other half', our 'better half' but that should stop. What I would like to say to myself is that you can only be who you truly are by being 100 per cent yourself, and that is enough. For only by being fully yourself and accepting yourself as good enough, can you be fulfilled. No-one else can do it for you. You need to love yourself first and feel complete.

So, to that girl in the mirror, I say you are enough. I stand beside you, and we talk, and this time we change what you said. You are beautiful inside and out, and you are not only enough, you are more than enough. There is no need to meet anyone else's expectations. You are whole. You are unique. You don't need to be like anyone else. You are strong and you will survive and thrive through all the hardships that will come. Everything is OK.

To that girl in the mirror, and to all the other men and women who look in the mirror and find themselves lacking in some way – stop. You are good enough just the way you are.

Don't let others determine what good enough is. You are always enough. There is no need to compare to others, comparing yourself to others is a recipe for dissatisfaction and distress. After all, you are unique and that is your gift to the world.

It is still okay to strive to be better, to learn more, and to do more. However, that doesn't detract from who you are today, that doesn't mean you are not good enough right now. To myself now, I say this, 'You are good enough, you are loved, you are perfect in every moment.'

Above all, there is no need to regret the paths untaken. The past cannot be changed, but the future is waiting for you to create it. So let go of any feelings of regret, say YES to as many opportunities as possible, and take the unknown path.

I am reminded again of one of my favourite quotes from Ralph Waldo Emerson, American philosopher and poet:

Do not go where the path will lead
Go where there is no path and leave a trail

Ralph Waldo Emerson (1803-1882)

It has taken me until my late fifties to really start to live those words. My past self was being led by others. It is now my time to leave that behind and make my own trail.

I am looking forward to the journey.

I Am The Key

Lisa Locks

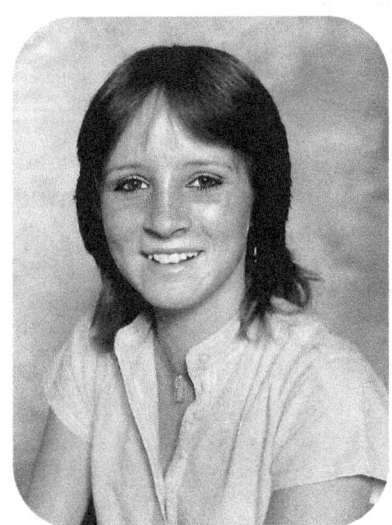

Caring and kind is always on my mind. Helping out a friend is what is really important, in the end.

Lisa Locks

As a 10-year-old girl, I found myself daydreaming a lot, which took my mind to many places. These daydreams were often mystical, but always had meaning – meaning I was yet to understand.

One specific daydream came to me time and time again. I could see myself sitting on top of an unbelievably beautiful mountain with a gigantic, gorgeous looking tree. With me, little Lisa sat dangling her legs over the edge, looking at the world from a height so far away. From this distance, the people below just looked like tiny ants scurrying around.

Everyone seemed to be in such a hurry, pushing and shoving like there was not enough time. The world down below looked as if it was passing by in a second, with the people living in such chaos. From a distance these tiny little ants had all the worries in the world, and I thought of the saying 'I feel like I am carrying the whole world on my shoulders.' I wondered; 'What are they thinking?' 'How do they feel?' 'What is important to them?'

Little Lisa, at the age of only 10, was already worried about everybody – everybody but herself. She had a seed in her right hand, and she chose to throw it over the edge. It landed on the ground and connected with the soil. There it was – a new tree was born. With the rain and the sun rays, it started to grow, just like me, as the jigsaw of my life unfolds.

My Story Begins

Although growing up with a family that truly loved me, everything wasn't perfect. Mum and Dad fought most of my life; they do still to this day, and I was always brought into it. They always wanted me to resolve their fights and take sides, 'Lisa, tell us whose fault it was.' 'Did your Mum say that?' 'Who do you think is telling the truth?' I wouldn't answer because no matter what I said, I would make one of them unhappy.

After years of trying to understand and not blaming myself, I felt like I was the ham in the sandwich. At times, I didn't know if I was the child or the adult in these situations. I felt my role in the family was to make everyone get along and be happy. You see, my background was one where some in my family were alcoholics and gamblers, and others suffered depression and anxiety. At the time, this didn't make much sense to me. All I thought was that I had to keep smiling, and that would make everyone happy. Maybe then there would be peace and tranquillity.

There were times when everyone was happy. Christmas day was always the highlight of my year. I always seemed to get what I wanted, and for some reason, Mum and Dad never fought on Christmas day.

Years later, when alcohol ruled my life, I never drank on Christmas day. It was a day of joy for me. Even now, Christmas is my favourite time of year.

At the age of seven I was diagnosed with chronic Bronchial Asthma which I struggled with most of my life. I missed a lot of school due to being very sick; sometimes three weeks at a time. Bronchitis and asthma would attack me, leaving me breathless, exhausted, and not sleeping for days on end, having to sit up as the coughing would not stop.

I would have to be on lots of medication such as antibiotics, preventatives, and cortisone which would make me very agitated and anxious. So, as I got older, I needed to be on the pump to help me breathe when I had asthma. It got quite scary at times. I felt as if someone was holding a pillow over my face and at any moment, I would stop breathing. My life felt threatened through this illness. It was very frightening as a child, not understanding the outcome of this illness, and even when the worst was over, it would take another two weeks to get over the exhaustion it caused.

This happened frequently. It was as easy as going out into the cold, being near dust, sitting on the grass or eating the wrong things – any of these could cause an attack. If I was asked to sleep at a friend's house, I would often get sick due to the environment. The simplest thing would trigger my asthma, even just getting excited or being worried about life in general. It just didn't take much for me to be sick. I was sick of being sick.

I remember at an early age, going from a Catholic primary school to a State high school; all the kids looked at me as if I had two heads. In a very short time, I was bullied, and it wasn't a nice feeling. Knowing what I know now, I can see how kids can be mean to each other, especially because of the competitiveness that seemed to exist between private and state schools.

I felt very alone and scared once again, and it was a very tough time of my life. Unfortunately, I ended up becoming a bully – and I'm not proud of that. People saw me as happy, but deep down, I was angry, and that made me a bully. I suppose I wanted to be a leader and feel important. If I could, I would take that back, but unfortunately it was my journey.

I can only tell my story and hope others think before they choose to become a bully. It's not a nice thing to do to others. Regrets and resentment is something I had to work on myself. I even had to go to see someone about this in my later years. I had to learn to let go and forgive myself and learn the reasons why I acted this way. My personal motto is now 'being kind is always on my mind.'

By the time I was 13, and in high school, I was already dabbling in alcohol and smoking cigarettes. I thought I had found me. I loved the taste, and it loved me, well, that's what I thought. I was now wearing a mask and pretending to be someone other than me. I didn't care about what the outcome could be. I was invincible. I was larger than life. I could be whoever I wanted to be. I could say and do what I wanted.

My drinking progressed as I got older, and my asthma got worse. I just wanted to crawl up and die at times. I missed out on so much school; to the point where I was failing. Luckily, my mother would do most of my assignments, and she often let me stay home when I was either sick or didn't want to go.

I didn't understand anything the teachers were teaching me. I was so far behind that I couldn't make up the time. So I became the class clown. There were so many incidents. Once a boy picked me up and put me on top of the lockers. I stayed there for a few hours, waving to the students and hiding from the teachers until the same boy took me down. Another time, I was kicked out of a German class for being disruptive and then climbed up the side of the portable and rested my head on the window sill. I was funny, and everyone laughed, even the teachers. I had already become clever enough to disguise my poor work-ethics so that no one would notice.

When I look back now, I can see that being the clown made me feel very special, even loved when I think about it. It was a nice feeling as it made me happy, but most of all, I thought nobody would notice how dumb I really was. Yes, dumb. I had labelled myself dumb!

To me, it was okay to be dumb. My brother and sister were academics. My Mum and Dad were always happy to hear that my siblings had achieved an A+ in their reports but as long as I had a C or D, my parents were happy. I felt they had labelled me dumb too. I got to the point where I often wagged school to cope with not having to be embarrassed about not fitting in.

By year 10, I was offered a hairdressing apprenticeship which I took without hesitation. I couldn't get out of school quickly enough. I had worked part-time from a very young age. Little me had already worked out what I could and couldn't do. 'Yes,' I thought, 'No more school, and now I can make some money!' Working for me was a good feeling. This was one of the most exciting times of my life. I was so enthusiastic and ready to learn everything as quickly as I could. I loved this job.

Now that I look back, I wish I had not labelled myself as dumb and wish I had asked for help. I just needed to be patient with myself. Being kind to others was always on my mind. I just needed to be kind and caring to myself.

My Next Journey Begins

The arguments between my mother and father didn't stop as I got older. They had both come to a decision that it would be better if they separated. This occurred a lot throughout my childhood. It had been an on and off relationship for all my life. I now know why I couldn't understand what being in love meant – they say monkey see monkey do. As an adult now, I can see that I had never learnt how to love. My parents didn't know how to love each other. I had no guidance, but I do realise that they did the best they could.

It took many years and experience to find out the true meaning of love – to love someone is to love oneself first. I did move out with my fiancé at the age of 21. For me, it was an escape. I was moving out to freedom as I thought it meant that I could do what I wanted. I had my own business at such a young age, a hairdressing salon, and life was looking good. I was making lots of money, loved my job, and most of all, I could drink whenever I wanted to.

One year into my marriage I was unsettled, confused and disconnected, so I decided to leave him. Most of my life I was confused and upset. I felt so alone, scared, sad, worried and most of all, in fear that I would get sick with asthma. I did go back to him. He was a great man. I just wasn't ready, but I stuck with him and did my best to make things right.

By the age of 26, I had my first baby, a girl. I had my salon, a husband and now a baby. The mask was on, yet I didn't understand at all what or where my life was heading. The next two years were excellent, and I had another child, a boy. I love kids as I can relate to them.

In some way, I felt I never grew up. I still don't think I have at times. I like to keep my childlike-minded ways. It makes me relate to my inner child, and helps me to relate to other children. I love all animals too. I see parts of my personality in all animals spiritually.

Time passed quickly as my kids were growing up. I love being a mum and I have a real bond with my two kids. My daughter is married to my beautiful son-in-law and she has two beautiful dogs. She is a hairdresser and works with me in our salon *Lisa's Locks Hairdressing*. I would have to say she is my rock and I am hers. My son is a loving and caring, beautiful soul. He wears his heart on his sleeve and is always watching over me, making sure I am safe. He has a great job and has such good work ethics. I am so proud of them both.

My children are my world and I do believe in my soul that I have tried to show them love and kindness, to be honest to themselves, and to love and cherish every moment they have. My two kids have a unique bond that they share and I hope they carry that through forever.

Self Discovery

But at the age of eight and ten, my children were watching me become unmanageable; my life was becoming unbearable due to my drinking. Alcohol took over my life.

Alcohol was the medicine to help me cope with my anxiety. Initially, drinking helped me to forget my anxiety but eventually, drinking was causing anxiety. I wanted to be a good parent, but all I could think about was my next drink. Eventually, drinking became a daily habit.

Even when I was getting ready to go out, I couldn't finish my shower without coming out several times to have a drink. I was completely out of control due to the drinking. It ruled my life. I was losing my soul. I had given up, and I was surrendering, hands up in the air.

At 35 years of age, I had to be taken away to a rehabilitation centre for 30 days for my alcoholism and drug habit; away from everybody, family and friends. I didn't understand. Where, who, and why? I was lost. Was I ever going to find myself again? It was there that I found my new beginnings. I began to learn more about myself. I discovered myself.

My counsellor in rehab told me that I had the mindset of a nine-year-old child. By the time I was ready to be dismissed, after 30 days, I had the mindset of a 30-year-old. That wasn't bad I thought; considering I was actually 35 and I had grown up in such a short time. I felt I had learnt something.

I had learnt that I was going away with my own tool kit to re-build my self-awareness and self-worth. I didn't realise then that it was going to take me another decade to catch on. The thing is, I knew right at that moment, looking back at my inner self as a child at 10 years old, that I was one day going to live by example and help children believe in themselves and follow their dreams. I followed my path of wellbeing and nurturing myself, gathering over the years as many mentors and healers as I could.

I am very grateful to have had a spiritual awakening. A spiritual teacher once said to me, 'Fake it till you make it, take one step at a time, take a deep breath and think before you speak.' That is exactly what I believed I needed to do, to experience what was right for me.

One day at a time and I would slowly but surely grow into the person I wanted to be and make my dreams come true. I knew at that point, I had to work hard at creating who I am and what I want in life, and that to me was simple. Keep it simple because I knew I was complicated at a very early age. I was different from others. I was unique, but I had a lot of wisdom to share, both then and now.

I believe I am on this journey to live and learn, and to give back what knowledge I have received from the experience of my own life, but not by pointing the finger. It's through living by example. They say when you point the finger, it points straight back at you. I'm now at a stage in my life, where there is never enough to learn. I don't ever want to miss out on all the dreams I have planned, as I did when alcohol ruled my life.

At this point in time, I look back and see everything I put out there is all coming back to me. You see, about 10 years ago I made a vision board that one day I would have a hairdressing salon again, but this time in my own home. This was so I could be creative and make people happy.

I now have a hairdressing salon that I love; getting up in the morning in the environment of my own home, I welcome clients into my salon, and it is truly well worth every moment. I get to learn from so many people, and most of all my interactions are with like-minded people.

They say you attract the people that are similar to you and I'm quite happy with that. I believe we can become whatever we want to become. Once upon a time, it seems so long ago but yet not so far away – as a child I had created my own identity, labelled myself as dumb and believed that everybody around me thought I was dumb. I was growing into an adult with no self-worth, no self-love, helpless, unwell, getting sicker as I got older.

Through self-discovery, I reinvented the little child from the adult form. By changing negativity into positivity, I can create the real Lisa and have the wisdom to know the difference. I am always willing to learn and discover more about health and well-being so that I can be an exemplary person for new generations. Therefore, I would like my freedom and belief system that I call 'my key to my toolset' to open the key to my heart so that I can love myself.

I Always Had the Key

Through knowledge, love and acceptance, I have created a key in my mind. This key has unlocked the negativity and self-doubt, which may sometimes occur. It is the simple steps that I take on a daily base. I call it the key to my toolset - in other words, the power of positive thinking and motivation. This improves my level of self-esteem as well as self-worth. The key to unlocking my self-belief and self-worth has always been within me.

My message to my inner child is to stay positive. Live with an open, warm heart. I am the master of my destiny through self-discovery and finding the courage to discover my self-trust. Through this discovery, I have experienced an abundance of self-worth that allows me to embrace self-love fully. I feel trust in myself and the world around me and thus, I experience emotional fulfilment and what I coin to be emotional success. For me, this has been life-changing.

Furthermore, my experiences of self-love and self-trust illuminate my inner awareness to trust not only myself but the greater world around me. These lessons and self-discoveries continue today.

The key to unlocking my self-belief and self-worth has always been within me, but it has taken me to look within myself to find it.

Now at 53 years old, I am still on this never-ending journey of learning to discover myself, my dreams, the wisdom to know the difference and to bring my dreams to life.

We all have a key inside us, a key that unlocks who we really are. I hope that my story inspires you to find and unlock the key to your heart.

Steven Up

Stefano D'Agata

How much of the child at seven is there in the man? Much of our personalities and values may be set in place at an early age, but we continue to grow, physically, mentally and spiritually throughout our lives, and this must count for something. But maybe, just maybe, the things that defined us in our youth are the very things that will bring us contentment in later life.

Stefano D'Agata

A Message To Your Younger Self

Seven:

Hey 7-year-old Steve. That's your name, isn't it?

Of course, you know yourself as *Steven* but, you haven't yet sighted your birth certificate which shows that your real name is *Stefano*. *Stefano* is a foreign name to you because no one has ever used it in your presence. Not even by your parents. They have always referred to you as *Steven*. So, there is no question that *Steven* is your name.

However, it is at this time in your life that you discover that *Steven* can also be written as *Stephen*. This is an intriguing revelation. Why get about as an ordinary old *Steven* when you could go by *Stephen*. *Stephen* has a more sophisticated edge to it, and you like that. So, from now on, when asked, 'How do you like to spell your name, with a *v* or a *ph*?' you choose the *ph* every time. Notwithstanding the fact that in your adult life, you will mostly introduce yourself as *Steve*, when writing your full name, you will always use *Stephen*. So, at a very young age, you are showing some nuance to your personality.

Your life otherwise seems unremarkable. Unremarkable to you, that is. Because of course, you don't know any different. You are one of six siblings; your parents were born in Egypt but speak Italian at home. You understand the Italian language but don't speak it much. Coming from a large migrant family is not unusual to you because almost everyone at the Catholic school you attend has parents born overseas and some kids have 10 or more siblings.

What is unusual to you though, is the references you see in some schoolbooks to *New Australians*. Isn't everyone in Australia, Australian? If there are *new Australians*, who are the old Australians? I recall you asked one of your teachers about this, but you didn't get a straight answer, did you?

Looking back, these actions and experiences are all signs of a clever inquisitive mind. Your creative mind and your need to differentiate yourself from others will see you well in future years.

Fourteen:

Here you are all grown up already. An early developer, you reached your adult height before you turned 13. Not sure where you fit in with the schoolyard tribes though. You're an 'A' grade student, and many of your closest friends could be considered *nerds*. You are definitely not a *jock,* but you are the school sprint champion for your age group and were very disappointed when the school didn't continue to have a field hockey team, as this was your preferred sport. But it is the thespian in you that is coming to the fore. In only your second year in the school musical production, you have scored a minor lead role and are starting to show some promise as a character actor. Sadly, you will eventually forego your desire to be a famous actor and follow a safer career path.

This decision will keep you wondering of what could have been as the desire to perform will never leave you. In future years you will see the same passion for following artistic pursuits in your children. Your advice to them then is to follow your dreams because ultimately, to achieve great things, you must be true to yourself. You will also realise that it is not too late to apply this advice to yourself.

Coming from a family of practising Catholics and having completed your primary school education within the Catholic Education system, you find yourself, in your third year at a secular high school, beginning to question what this whole religion business is about. Hardly any of your friends are regular churchgoers, even the ones who went to Catholic primary schools. So, you're wondering, why do I need to go to church? To your credit though, rather than taking the easy route by walking away or alternatively, just going through the motions to keep the parents happy, you decide to investigate further before throwing it away.

You go on a youth retreat organised by the local parish and meet a nun who is on the hunt for young people to work as catechists. Catechists are people within the church who take on the task of teaching religious education to primary school-aged students who do not go to Catholic School. In short, you are to become a Sunday school teacher.

Unbeknown to you, this is a rare moment in time for the Catholic Church where, only just over a decade on from the second Vatican Council, priests and nuns are taking full advantage of newfound freedoms to explore progressive ideas and modern interpretations of scripture. Alas, you will eventually discover that this period was an all too brief aberration in the history of Roman Catholicism and conservative forces within the church would eventually try to stifle such liberties.

But for now, you are being introduced to a very progressive education in Christianity and at an adult level. This was a far more rounded and comprehensive religious education than you could ever have hoped to achieve had you stayed within the Catholic school system. The belief systems you develop now, such as how the church is first and foremost a congregation of people and God is essentially our collective consciousness, not unlike *The Force* in *Star Wars*, will stay with you for the rest of your life.

But something really big happens in your 14th year, and this is something that you never really come to terms with. At the age of only 53, one Friday night in late November, your father has a heart attack and dies. The way you respond to this has puzzled me to this day. You seem to take it in your stride. But have you really? Your uncle, Dad's older brother, had also died of a heart attack only a few months earlier. So, you obviously thought that it was not unusual that your dad could go the same way. You look to your faith for justification and resolve that God wanted him, so God took him away. But for Christ's sake man! Your dad just died! This is huge! He's left your 46-year-old mother widowed with seven children aged between six and 20. What a terrible thing to happen.

You don't cry or can't cry; I don't know which. It will take you another 16 years for you to release your emotions. That's mainly because you finally have someone you are comfortable crying with. But at that time, at that place, although you had many to share your grief with, you wanted to keep it to yourself. You didn't want to draw attention to it and didn't want people to feel sorry for you. But looking back at it now, I feel sorry that this terrible thing had to happen to you and your family.

Sadly, fate will give you another opportunity to deal with the tragic loss of a loved one. You'll do a bit better that time. But I only wish you would have known that it was okay to grieve and that you had a right to be sad and a right to cry. Holding it in did not help, did it?

Twenty-one:

Welcome to adultery... err, I mean adulthood. Congratulations, at the end of high school you chose the safe career path and enrolled in a Civil Engineering Degree. So why are you working full-time in a petrol station?

Whether Civil Engineering didn't like you or you didn't like it, I don't know. But after two years at university, you only completed one year of study and decided that perhaps it was time for a gap year. You'd been working part-time at a petrol station for over a year when the opportunity arose to go full time. Your talent and intellect didn't go unnoticed with your employer though, and after a year of working behind the console at a self-service site, he decides to buy another site and wants you to run it.

So, at the age of 21, you are managing a small business and have taken a small loan against your mother's house to buy a 10 per cent stake in it. This proves to be a very profitable exercise, but it's not really a career is it? So, after two years pumping gas, you resolve to return to university and complete your degree. But, at least now you are not a struggling student anymore. You have a relatively large sum of money in the bank and continued part-time employment as a day manager on weekends. Well done you.

During your second gap year, you also take the opportunity to move out on your own for a bit. You find a great bed-sit apartment just opposite the Carlton Gardens in Melbourne and set up your own bachelor pad. Not that this really helps you much with the ladies though. Don't know what will help you with the ladies. You don't seem to know how to initiate relationships and, for all your intelligence, you don't have the capacity to recognise when someone may be interested in you. One of your best friends is a total chick magnet and seems to be able to crack onto anyone, anywhere he goes. But you are not him.

It's not that you are overly shy, it's just that you are forever worried about starting something you can't finish. Others seem to be able to go in and out of casual relationships, but you can't contemplate it. You think that there is something wrong with you. But maybe you're just not a one-night stand kind of guy and are looking for a meaningful relationship. There's nothing wrong with that, but you must start somewhere fella, and you just don't know how to kick things off. The sad news is, that you still don't.

How's that religion thing going? Oh well, like most people born into the Roman Catholic faith, you have become what is known as a *lapsed Catholic*. It is about this time that you start to describe yourself as a *lapsed Catholic* but *born-again* Christian. Not the best description you could have come up with because you're not *born-again* in the *Hallelujah* speaking in tongues sense. It's more that the fundamentally progressive Christian beliefs you developed in your teenage years have not left you.

Twenty-eight:

Sweet 28 and never been kissed. Not entirely true, but it may as well be. Still can't get the relationship thing going. You have a couple of starts but end up falling at the first hurdle. Yes, you are an intuitive person and have a good sense as to what others are thinking or feeling. But you expect that mutual understanding will be enough to establish a relationship. You fail to recognise that others do not share your intuition, so you need to use words and actions to get things happening.

It's not like you are wanting for social opportunities. You have a strong group of friends with whom you have regular outings and weekends away, but you're still just too stupid to pick up on signals that others may be interested in you. Don't give up hope, though. Your lonely days will be over sooner than you think. But not just yet.

You made the right decision to go back to university to complete your degree. You have a secure job with a state government-owned water corporation and, although you don't realise it, you are working at the forefront of modern asset and infrastructure management and are setting the groundwork for a great career in this area of engineering. The job pays well too, and within less than three years, you managed to save enough to buy your first home.

Congratulations! Of course, you can't afford to live in it yet but, you've made a solid investment in a 2-bedroom semi-detached house in inner Melbourne.

Your spiritual development hasn't progressed much from when you were 21. You still have the same belief system, but you prefer to go to the gym on Sunday mornings rather than go to church. You have not yet reconciled yourself with the Catholic Church but watch this space. They haven't seen the last of you.

Thirty-five:

Well, look at you now. Who would have thunk it? You're happily married and living in the house you bought eight years prior with your wife Maria and, you're a daddy to boot. You were introduced to Maria by mutual friends in late 1992. You managed to overcome your propensity towards procrastination this time and followed through to enter a serious relationship.

By the time you turned 30 you were an item and almost two years to the day since you met, you got married. Not three years later, just when you both agreed that it was time to start a family, you found out that you already had and in October 1997, your first child was born – a beautiful little girl who will give you both joy and pain in equal doses for many years to come.

You and Maria are an excellent match. You both have reputations for appearing quiet and shy on first impressions, but once people get to know you, you both reveal your mischievous side. Like all good relationships, you have your differences too. But these only enhance your compatibility.

Maria's conservative Catholic upbringing could have clashed with your progressive one. But what it did, is bring you back into the church fold. Once you are back in, you can't help but get involved. The reforms of the second Vatican Council are having one last hurrah, and someone in the Diocese has decided that local parishes need a *Pastoral Council*.

A *Pastoral Council* consists of a group of parishioners who work with the Parish Priest to see to the pastoral needs of the congregation. Not the practical needs, but the pastoral needs. So, lay-people are now being encouraged to have a say on how the word of God is spread within the congregation.

In your local inner Melbourne parish, you and Maria get involved in the inception of the *Pastoral Council* and you become an inaugural member. But, that's not all. You seem to be exuding leadership qualities you didn't know you had, and the *Council* has elected you as its inaugural chair. In addition to this, you and Maria reinvigorate the parish youth group, and you both get involved with assisting with special liturgical celebrations. This provides an opportunity for the actor in you to escape from its shackles. For three years running, you take on the role of Pontius Pilot in the Easter *Passion Play* to rave reviews.

So, here you are, married to a beautiful wife with a beautiful daughter and an active spiritual existence. Work is going fantastically as well. You are in middle-management and still working at the forefront of asset and infrastructure management. Life is good.

Forty-two:

My God, you're a country boy! In mid-1999, you decide to take a new job with a water corporation in a regional town 200km north of Melbourne. This is a much smaller corporation than the one you previously worked with, and you now have almost sole responsibility for water supply and sewerage network planning and asset management for 50 communities.

The town where you work has a population of 30,000, but this is not enough of a country experience for Maria and yourself. So, you make your home in a much smaller town which is only a 20-minute commute to work. This town consists of about 100 houses, a shop, a school, a kindergarten and a pub. You've set yourself up for an idyllic lifestyle in an idyllic place. The sale of your house in Melbourne has allowed you to pay cash for your country home which is almost three times bigger and on a 12 times bigger allotment.

Maria has given up her career in the rag-trade to make the move with you, and you both justify this on the basis that you want to grow the family. It doesn't take you too long to do this as just over a year after the move, your second daughter arrives.

Another two years pass, and your debt-free existence allows you to take a long-awaited overseas holiday. This trip was extremely important to Maria who, at the impressionable age of 16, emigrated from Malta to Australia with her parents and siblings. Sixteen years on, Maria dearly wanted to return to her homeland to see her old friends and especially, her grandmother. So, with your four-year-old and two-year-old daughters in tow, you pack your bags for a seven-week holiday to Malta and get to spend time in Italy and London as well. A great adventure and a great reunion for Maria and her grandmother, who would sadly die of old age the following year.

You departed Australia as a family of four but returned as a family of five, as nine months later your son was born. Your family is now complete. You will often go on to claim that the secret to having a son after two daughters is reverse polarity. You must conceive on the other side of the globe.

Religion is still a big deal for Maria and yourself. For you, just attending services was never enough. Your new parish also has a *Pastoral Council,* and it is not long before you become a member of it and guess what? Before your time in the country is up, you will be elected as chair of that *Council* as well.

Your involvement with this country parish is a milestone in your spiritual development, as it is led by a truly fabulous progressive parish priest. He not only reinvigorates the belief systems you've carried since your teenage years; he calls them into action. Sadly, it is during your time at this parish that you first discover the lengths to which conservative forces within the church will go to stifle such liberties. But, for the moment, the good guys are winning.

You've got a great full life in a great community with a great family. But you feel that you need to progress your career. The country job was always seen as a stepping stone to other things, and it is in your 42nd year that you find work back in Melbourne as an Engineering Consultant. A better paid more prestigious job for sure, but was it worth giving up such a great lifestyle? In the end, it was all just part of the journey, and you really needed to be back in Melbourne to deal with the trials that you will soon have to endure.

Forty-nine:

Your return to Melbourne was meant to be the start of bigger and better things. Career-wise, this had panned out better than expected. Within a couple of years, you are promoted to head the infrastructure planning and asset management department in the Melbourne office of a multi-national consultancy firm. This sees you managing over 30 staff delivering significant projects up and down the east coast of Australia. To date, this remains the high point of your engineering career.

Pining for the country home you left behind, you and Maria decide to purchase a property on a bush acre on the outskirts of Melbourne. Your budget is enough to provide the space and serenity you both desire but, the house on the site is significantly smaller than the one you left behind, is riddled with termites and infested with rats. But never mind, with your family complete, Maria can re-enter the workforce, and with two salaries you should be able to raise the funds needed to build your dream home on your dream site.

Sadly, this wasn't to be. A year after your return and only a couple of months after purchasing your new home, Maria notices a lump in her breast. Within a week she is in hospital having a mastectomy and chemotherapy commences shortly afterwards.

Your hopes for a lasting remission are dashed when three years later, secondary cancers are discovered. More chemo keeps this at bay for another two years before tumours in the brain are discovered and you realise that it is the beginning of the end. The start of your 49th year sees Maria in palliative care, and by mid-April of that year, her battle is lost.

This time you cry. You cry like you never cried before. But you quickly must dry your tears because you are now sole parent to three wonderful kids, the eldest of which is the same age that you were when your father died. The significance of this is not lost on you, and you make sure that your children know that it is okay to grieve. Whilst you provide them with the space to do this, you know that you have already been in a state of grief for several years.

You think that after a short holiday you will be ready to move on with your lives. Didn't quite work out that way, did it? You discovered that grief takes various forms and all you have done is move from one state of grief to another. For all the time you knew she was dying; she was still there. In fact, it was only the last few months of her life that she was seriously incapacitated.

So, in practice, you had been living a normal existence albeit within the shadow of an impending tragedy. But it is only now that she is gone that you feel true loss and you're not prepared for it. All the support you had around you during those last few months is gone too. People offered continued assistance, but you sent them away. You reasoned that you couldn't keep relying on others indefinitely, but now you are all alone.

Religion is still there for you. As with your previous parishes, it didn't take long for Maria and yourself to get involved in various groups and activities. Once again, you ended up on the *Pastoral Council* and once again you eventually get elected as chair. Initially, the parish you belong to is an exemplary example of progressive Catholicism.

You will soon discover however, that all is not well. Conservative forces within the church have sent spies to your Parish. These spies, known as the *Temple Police*, discovered that your parish was taking liberties with the doctrines of the *Holy Roman Catholic Church*. A deliberate decision was made by the Diocese to quash blasphemous acts such as singing parts of the Mass that should be spoken, having lay members of the congregation deliver homilies and promoting reconciliation services as an alternative to individual confessions.

You and your progressive counterparts have been put back in your place. Congratulations, you are now officially part of *the resistance.*

You channel your anger and bitterness with the church hierarchy into writing your religious manifesto. This manifesto starts life as a satirical novel about the Papacy, but you use satire and comedy to explore the juxtaposition between the hierarchical church, who are the last bastions of the *Holy Roman Empire*, and the true faithful who believe and follow Christ's message of respect and love for all people and all things. You fantasise that the publication of this work will bring you fame and fortune as well as infamy.

In your time of need though, the true church, your true church, is there for you. So, in acknowledgement of the wealth of support you got from the local church and school community during Maria's illness and passing, you write the following:

My church has no windows,
but it is always full of light.
My church has no doors,
but people come and go as they please.
My church has no roof,
but the wind and rain never get in.
My church is built from the love and faith
of a community that cares.
My church has no windows,
but God's love shines through every day.

Fifty-six:

Here we are, all caught up. Looking back at my life in seven year segments has been very cathartic. I have discovered that the spiritual beliefs I developed in my youth, have only been reinforced over the years. It is also clear however, that I have suffered more than my fair share of adversity. I guess no one is immune to adversity, but I seem to have suffered more blows than most. But I got through, and I am still here.

As you can imagine, the past seven years have been a struggle. An international buy-out of the consultancy firm I worked for resulted in my role within the organisation being severely diminished. So, soon after Maria's passing, I decided to leave. I thought I might make a go of it as an independent consultant, but no one seemed to be interested. By early 2013, the little life insurance money I had received from Maria's superannuation began to dry up, and I had to find a job, any job. Thus, commenced my career in local government.

After initially accepting a low-grade role, I have gradually regained some managerial responsibility. The salary still does not match what I was earning at my peak, and this, along with the late realisation that becoming a single parent sent me a few rungs down on the socio-economic ladder, led to serious financial difficulties which almost cost me my house. I am crawling out of the mire as we speak, but it is a slow crawl.

The vision for the house we bought soon after returning to Melbourne, was never realised. This caused Maria a lot of distress in her final months. But I had to let it go as it was too much for me to maintain and too inconvenient for the kids to make their own way to school and social activities. Consequently, the house didn't fetch a good price, but I was able to purchase another home close to the kids' high school and on a local bus route. All this required committing to a hefty mortgage, so it is no wonder that my personal financial position was severely challenged.

Maria's death also took a psychological toll on me and my three children. Three of us are actively being treated for illnesses associated with depression and anxiety, but the fourth one wants to soldier on and focus on getting on with her life. Wonder where she gets that from? You will need to read my chapter in the forerunner to this book titled *Live Your Truth* to find out more about this. But in short, we are managing, if only just.

The lessons learnt in recent years have also taught me that life is too short not to do the things you love. I still get angry at my wife Maria for not doing enough for herself in her final years. She lived a selfless life committed to being of benefit to others. I knew she resented this, but she still wouldn't take the time to do things for herself. I have now learnt that we are of no good to others unless we look after ourselves.

So, in recent years, I have pushed myself to do the things I want. This includes exercising my writing skills and working towards getting my novel published. I would love it to be a critically acclaimed financial success, but even if it isn't, I recognise that it is a massive achievement to publish an 80,000-word manuscript which I know will bring enjoyment and enlightenment to more than a few people. I have also acted on my desire to perform by posting material on YouTube and writing and performing stand-up comedy. Friends say it is courageous of me to do this, but really, at 56, what have I got to lose.

Religion wise, without Maria's devoutness and dedication, I am afraid that I have become a lapsed Catholic again. Now I refer to myself as a religious fundamentalist. Not in the radicalised sense of the term though. I guess I should say that I am really a spiritual fundamentalist because I fervently believe that all religions are based on the same fundamental spiritual beliefs.

Those beliefs are that we are all part of, or owe our allegiance to, a higher power and our combined worth is greater than the sum of our parts. All religions are based on this fundamental belief and all religions believe that, because of this belief, we need to respect the needs and wishes of others, prevent the exploitation of our environment and give thanks for the world we live in and the people, plants and animals we share it with.

Looking back, what I've learnt is that we need to do these things not just because it is good to be nice to other people, but because we cannot separate ourselves from the entity we belong to and we must be good to ourselves.

Think of it like *The Force* in *Star Wars*.

Somewhere Over The Red Sky

Christine Carmuciano

A bird sitting on a tree is never afraid of the branch breaking because its trust is not in the branch but in its own wings.

(Author Unknown)

As I walk along the sands of this familiar beach, I watch and listen as the tide gently makes its way back to the shore. The sky is turning a beautiful blue with shades of pink, reminiscent of the day that was and the promise of the day to come.

As I sit here, it conjures up a fond memory of my mother, and I can't help but remember something she would always say, 'Rosso di sera, bel tempo si spera!' which meant that when the night sky was red, there was hope for beautiful weather the next day.

My mind is cast back to a time I would sit on this very beach, pensive and planning what my life might look like in the years to come. Unknowingly wishing my life away for a so-called independence I thought I needed. Yet life has taken a full circle for me now, and I find myself thinking the same thoughts, as again, I walk along this very same beach, alone.

Although this time I am not in my teens, I am in my mid-fifties. I suppose that young girl inside of me is still there, still searching and planning what her future might look like now.

If I have to go back in time to the exact moment when I decided to assert myself as an independent female, my mind takes me back to when I was approximately eight years old.

My father owned a property with his brother, and one Saturday morning I accompanied him, as I quite often did. My older cousin was painting the wall in one of the rooms that needed repair, and I asked my father if I could help him. My father said, 'No, this isn't a job for a girl!' Not unreasonable you might say, being that I was only eight years old, but who was to know that those words would remain ingrained in me till this very day!

This was the creation of the story in my head.

Those simple words, destructive and motivating at the same time, would be the catalyst that would shape my personality and drive through the years. They would, in essence, become my mantra, 'I'll show you. I can do anything I want to!'

This mantra that was born from a time when I was so young, has ended up ruling me, all of my life. Always feeling the need to prove myself as a female, that I can do anything I put my mind to and that my gender is not going to determine what I can and can't do.

If there is one thing I wish I knew then as I do now, is that I didn't have to spend my whole life trying to prove myself. When all the while, I was loved regardless, and my worth had nothing to do with whether I was a girl or a boy.

The irony of the 'painting' saga, call it Karma if you wish, is that painting became a common chore for me throughout the years.

Separated in my early thirties with two young children, with no partner to turn to when it came to the upkeep of the family home, the work fell on to me. That old saying, 'Be careful what you wish for', reigns so true with me! I was so adamant that I could do it all on my own that in the end, it became a cross I would bear for most of my adult life. I am now in my mid-fifties and would be quite happy not to have to pick up a paintbrush ever again.

I spent so much time trying to prove myself, that I was as good as any male and could do it all on my own, that I forgot how to accept help in many instances. I took it to the extreme and felt it was a weakness in me if I did.

To this day, I am still working on asking for a hand, and even when I do, most times it is in exchange for something I can do for that person. I still feel quite uncomfortable in just saying 'Yes, that would be great!' and not feeling guilty about it.

How is it that these simple words from my father so long ago, could impact me so greatly my entire life and shape who I am and have been all these years?

As an adult, I can now see that those words were not said in malice or in a derogatory manner. They were purely from a place of what my father thought to be right and as a consequence of his upbringing and environment. Those words were actually from a place of love. He didn't want his little girl to come to any harm or have to do any 'hard' jobs.

To this day, he is still trying to protect me, take care of me and keep me from harm's way. With tears in his eyes, he looks at me and expresses his words and emotions in a way that he was never able to in my younger years.

As a teenager and the only girl in the family, I was always butting heads with my father. He was from the 'old school', strict and commanding and expecting us to obey without any questions. I was fiercely trying to establish my rights and independence in a home where my father was the breadwinner and my dear mother, the caregiver and homemaker. Although don't get me wrong, my mother was a very strong woman who always said what she thought and would more often than not be the one to smooth the path between myself and my father.

What I realise now as a grown woman, is that I always thought I had to battle with him in trying to prove myself, but in fact he was only trying to be my protector, and still is. He has been the only man who has been a constant in my life and shown me nothing but unconditional love. He has been there for me through all my trials and been a testament to what a true family man is. He has always shown me strength and guidance, and even though I resented it so many times in the past, I now know it was always from a place of love, support and protection.

I love my father dearly, but to be honest as a teenager, I would have found it very hard to express those feelings. I now look at my 94-year-old father who has endured so much in recent times, the sudden loss of his eldest son and his soul mate of more than 65 years, my beautiful mother.

I look at him with so much admiration and compassion, a man who has been so devoted to his family his whole life. If only that little eight-year-old girl knew then, what she knows now! Maybe her mantra would have been different.

Over the past few years, especially since turning 50, I have pondered on my life, still searching, always searching. For what? I'm still to answer that, but maybe it's just living life to the fullest and not taking everything to heart and letting it rule your life.

Did those words so long ago really shape my life, cause a trigger in my mind that said I had to prove my worth and my independence in every decision and action I took? Was I, in fact, the only person who made my life harder than what it needed to be? The decisions I made alone, shaped my life and made it one of many hurdles.

If I truly reflect on my teenage years, it can be quite confronting and painful at times. I'm not sure where my head was at during those years, but I do know that my story was certainly gaining momentum and if I look back now, I probably made some very questionable decisions, as I imagine we could all probably relate to when we look back on our younger years.

I chose to leave school mid-way through year 12, because I thought it would be great to become a hairdresser. I only decided this after a conversation with a distant cousin who I thought was very cool. Well, she had to be, all the boys liked her! And so, I embarked on a new journey, one that was so different from what I had been preparing myself for all my years at school. I left my comfort zone and friends I had known for many years, to venture out on my own.

Graduating, I found out quite quickly that it was not all I had fantasised and that I was in a job that wasn't me. I hated every day that I had to go to work. It was also at this time that I had fallen in love with my future husband. I was 16. It should have been an exciting and liberating time in my life, yet I felt conflicted in my choices.

I tried my hardest to suck it up and get on with it and not disappoint my parents. After all, I was the one who was so determined in my choice to leave school, even though they had their reservations. I tried to fit in, but knew I wasn't being my authentic self. A feeling I sometimes still struggle with. I can be with friends and still feel like I don't belong. My emotions were out of control. I was in love but hated my life. It was not what I had dreamt it would be!

Thoughts of not wanting to be around anymore entered my head more than once, a story in my head I could not shake. What was I doing? Who was I? I remember walking across the road one day, consciously not looking, hoping that a car would hit me. It wasn't that I didn't want to be around, but in hindsight, it was a call for help or maybe that inner child of mine was calling out that she wasn't ready to be out on her own and just wanted a hug! But of course, I wouldn't listen. I was on my quest to be an independent woman at all costs!

I felt I couldn't talk to anyone and that no-one understood me. Inside I was spiralling downward, although on the outside, most would not have known.

My quest for independence at such a young age led me to be married at 19. I thought this would be the answer to all my problems. That being on my own, in control of my own life and not having to answer to anyone, would be my saviour. Or so I thought!

It was just the beginning of the next 30 years of my life that would be my hardest in so many ways - physically, emotionally, financially and mentally. In every aspect, it certainly was a rollercoaster of a ride! My guiding lights through all of it, and ones that I would never replace, are my two amazing children, now young adults.

How ironic that at this very time I find myself putting pen to paper, my children are now 30 and 33. The exact time when my married life as I knew it, started to unravel, yet theirs is just beginning. They are now embarking on their future with their incredible partners, yet at that same age, I felt that mine was ending.

A lifetime lived at 33!

Married at such a young age, I learnt about responsibilities and commitment very quickly. There was no time for frivolity or being carefree; a mortgage to pay and bills to tackle, I became an instant 'grown-up'.

I chose to take the path that I thought I needed to become an 'adult', which in turn would bring this so-called 'independence' I had been longing for. But in doing so, I walked away from my childhood. I cut my teenage years short and hadn't even started to explore who I was and wanted to be as an independent woman. How ironic, when all I wanted to be was an independent woman!

Instead, I fell in love. I turned my back on my dreams of travelling and exploring the world and what I wanted for myself. What I truly felt deep down in my soul, I quashed! Any signs that I saw, I ignored.

In a way, I cannot blame my ex-husband. He was young at the time also, only 21 and maybe he had his own dreams he wanted to aspire to, or his own journey still to travel. We just didn't know it at the time. We thought our young love was enough and it would endure a lifetime.

I cannot speak for him and cannot claim to know where his mindset was at, especially during the last five years of our marriage, which for me were the hardest. He decided to become an interstate truck driver, convincing me that he was 'doing it for the family' and that it would be better in the long run for our financial position. Instead, it just brought about many lonely nights, very heated arguments about where all the money was going, which ultimately nearly sent us bankrupt. But still, I naively believed everything he told me and found myself questioning decisions I had made and wondering many times; 'If only?'

I have a very vivid memory of an evening, where I stood at a pivotal crossroad in my life. He happened to be outside and had left his phone on the kitchen bench; a rare occurrence as it was normally by his side 24/7. The phone rang and it was a woman on the other end, asking to speak with him.

I will never forget the way his face changed when I said, 'So & so is on the phone for you.' My heart sank when he stepped outside to take the call. Was this the beginning of the end? Was I so naive to the fact that he was being unfaithful and for how long? A million thoughts ran through my mind at the same time. I will never forget the 'Judas' hug he gave me when he came back inside, reassuring me that I was being silly and that he would never hurt me!

I knew he was lying, but I also knew that if I stood my ground and caused a scene, the life I had known for the past 14 years and the life I had created with him and my two beautiful children, would be over. Just like that! In a microsecond, my life as I knew it would never be the same.

I cowered. My comfort zone, as bad as it had become, was all I knew. I couldn't bear the thought that my marriage might be coming to an end. Where would I find the strength to go it alone?

But in the end, the inevitable happened regardless. With trust forever lost and as a consequence, an irreparable marriage, I was left a single mother for most of my children's young lives. I suppose the responsibility caught up with him too and a promise of greener pastures and a carefree lifestyle, proved more tempting than a 'nagging' wife and the responsibilities that came with being a father and having a family.

I recently came across something I wrote back in 1997, titled; 'Ode to my Marriage' when my heart was still so raw from my breakup, and I was at the lowest of my lows. It's amazing how something you read or a song you hear, can take you right back to that place where you were and make you feel those same emotions all over again. To this day I still find it hard to listen to *Unbreak my Heart* by Toni Braxton and *Don't Speak*, by No Doubt. I would listen to these songs over and over again, tears streaming down my face. Would I ever get over this pain I was feeling? Would I ever be able to pick myself up from this deep dark well? I would pray that time would fly by just so that I didn't have to feel this pain anymore.

My ode demonstrates how much we can put on a show for everyone else, but then retreat to our own private deep, dark corner and feel totally alone and no-one would be the wiser. In a world where we are so busy and can become quite oblivious to others around us, maybe we can just check in every now and then and maybe we ourselves can reach out and not feel that we're bothering someone if we do. It doesn't always require words, it may just be a hug or someone to hold your hand for a time.

So this is a small part of what I wrote in one of my deepest, darkest moments:

You see everyone around you with their families together, husbands who love and care for them, an existence of normality you long for, but know that you can never have again.

And they say to you to be strong. Huh! They don't know how your heart is breaking, but you try not to let it show for fear it might allow a sign of weakness. So they go on and think that you are coping and let jokes of their intimacy fly, but inside you're dying, but you wouldn't dare let it show.

You laugh along with them and pretend that it's all okay, for it's not their fault that they have someone who loves them and you don't. So you hold it all inside, until late at night, when you're all alone, and your children are fast asleep. That's when you let down your guard and cry yourself to sleep and continually ask yourself that question, which no-one can answer; Why?

Sometimes I think of my life like the movie, *Sliding Doors*, starring Gwyneth Paltrow – choices that are made at a particular time in your life can take you down a very different path than may otherwise have been. You find yourself standing at a crossroads, you make the choice to take one path, but what would it have looked like if you had taken the other path instead? What would my life have looked like if I hadn't married so young? If I had chosen the career path I had been studying for? If I had worked overseas the way I had always dreamt I would? But then I wouldn't have the two most loving and inspiring people in my life that are my world, nor be blessed with the role of a grandmother to the most precious little boy. And it is these amazing people in my life that I know have made every decision I did make back then, all worthwhile!

The most obvious message to my young self here, would probably be, 'Don't get married so young!' But that's too easy, and I'm not sure if that is the right thing to say. When you fall in love, especially at such a young age, it consumes your whole world and the thought that 'happily ever after' might not eventuate, would never have been believed.

I would also want to reassure that young woman, that it's not your fault that you didn't see the signs or maybe didn't want to see the signs. Don't be so hard on yourself. An unfaithful partner can feel humiliating and make you question your self-worth. Was I not good enough, not pretty enough anymore? Was I such an awful wife? Was it all my fault? Why did my husband stray and my marriage break up when all my friends' marriages were still intact? What did I do differently from all of them?

I say to her, don't torture yourself and compare yourself constantly, it was just your journey, not theirs and above all, it was your husband's journey and the path he chose to take. Let go of the regret and anger, as I know you now have, even though it took a lot of soul searching to get here. Let go of anger and guilt when it comes to your children too. I know that you feel so guilty that maybe you didn't pick the 'right' father for them or that they deserved to have a father who was there by their side. That is true. They did deserve a loving father! But their journey has also made them who they are today, and you should be so proud of that and so should they.

I promise you also that this time shall pass. You will awaken from this emotional coma and climb out of this deep dark well you find yourself in at the moment. Know that it is just that, a 'moment' in all your years of life. One day you will wake up and decide 'No more! No more do I want to feel like a victim. Enough!' Know that it is at this very moment, when you decide to no longer define yourself as a victim, that the shackles of misery that have bound you will be released. Your inner strength will truly come to you when you recognise this and take back control. It is this very day your life is reborn, and you begin to heal, find yourself and create once more.

Now be proud of the woman you have become, hold your head up and know that you are an individual and there is no need to feel less a woman because you no longer have a husband in your life.

Don't measure your self-worth by the relationships you've had. Remember how many times you've had to recreate yourself over the years and stand tall because of it. Maybe it's time now to let the guard down because you are worthy of love. I can only reassure you that no matter what happens, you'll find your strength and you'll come through the other side, a stronger version of your prior self.

As if those tumultuous years weren't enough, the roller coaster ride wasn't over yet. I found myself having to draw on that strength all over again.

The Big C came along a few years after that. Breast cancer hit me out of the blue! I felt healthy, so how could cancer be eating its way inside of me? Sitting in the doctor's surgery on my own, I remember hearing the diagnosis; it was like an out-of-body experience. Again, my stubborn, independent self, thought I could handle this on my own. I can still remember sitting in the car in the doctor's car park after my appointment, crying uncontrollably, but then making sure I held it together before going home to my children. It was so surreal! Could this actually be happening to me?

Before I knew it, I was operated on and had to undergo a course of treatment which spanned the next five years of my life.

My bravado held up even at a time in my life where I could have allowed myself some 'weakness', but I continued to work through all of my treatment, only taking the days off when my nausea was so bad I couldn't get out of bed. To this day, I still struggle to say that I am a Cancer Survivor! Although of course, I am so grateful that I am, when so many others are not.

If there is anything I have learnt from my life and would want to reassure my younger self; it is that what doesn't break you, makes you! That there'll be times throughout your life where you will hit the lowest of the low, but it is these times where you will find strength in yourself that you never thought possible and you will rise above. Because rise above you will, as long as you have the courage to reach deep within yourself, but also be willing to reach out to others around you.

No one can read your mind, so don't be too proud or afraid to ask for help. Oh! And don't let your ego get in the way either, you're not being weak! Just remember that the load is much lighter when you let someone help you carry it.

And it's ok to show your vulnerable side; it will just bring you closer to the people around you and help break down the barriers. Know that you deserve to be loved and allow the people around you to love you. I know that when I did allow friends and family in, it sure did help and the feeling of being alone, was certainly lifted.

The Big One – don't always believe your own story, sometimes the words you tell yourself can do you more harm than good. Share what's going on inside of you. You might find that it's not so bad and that the story you've believed and told yourself for such a long time is just that, a story! A story that you can close the book on whenever you choose, instead of repeating it in your head over and over again, thereby ultimately becoming a prisoner to it, stopping you from moving on and breaking out of the cell you created for yourself.

Most importantly, never forget to feed that inner child and never stop laughing and dancing stupidly every moment you can. One of my fondest memories is of myself with my son and daughter, dancing crazily around our lounge room, letting loose without a care and laughing so hard our jaws hurt. These were our happy days, and even now my heart is filled to the brim whenever I remember.

You know I would tell my mother off because she laughed at what I thought were serious moments. I would become annoyed, thinking it was embarrassing. But you know, I think she knew the secret, laugh as much as you can! The world, our world, my world needn't be that serious. Find the lighter side of life, not the harder and darker side. Make lemonade out of lemons, as corny as that sounds. Life will always play hardball with you, but maybe you can find the fun in the game and not just focus on the rules and how it should or shouldn't be.

Don't be so hard on your parents either, your relationship with them, especially when you are a teenager, can be very misunderstood. Just remember, as teenagers, lots of times we resent our parents because we believe they don't understand us or they have no idea what we're going through. But believe me, they do. They were once your age and had their own issues and battles to go through and parents who they felt didn't understand them. We are all bi-products of our environment, but it's up to us, as individuals to change that if we want, not just blame them because we think we have the right.

I know that this is what I battled with the most growing up living in my parent's home. I wish that you, my younger self, would have known that these very same battles you struggled with your parents, would be the same ones that you would struggle with your teenage children growing up, and I am sure they will, in turn, struggle with theirs. I remember my mum saying to me, 'You wait till you have your own children, then you'll see!' She was so right!

Don't be so hard on yourself. I can reassure you that you did the best you could, you always have and you always will.

Remember this is not a new stigma; it is one that every generation will experience, not just you, the battle between child and parent. It is only when you become a parent yourself that you will realise how important the role is, that fine line between being a parent and a friend. Trying to make sure you instil the right values and morals that will lay the foundations to keep them in good stead all their lives. Hoping they will make the right decisions and not be afraid to stand out from the crowd. To not be a follower just because it's easier, but instead, to rise above and have the courage to be a leader and most importantly, to always follow their intuition and gut instinct.

Your intuition is your biggest sign if things are right or wrong – if it doesn't feel right, then it isn't!

My story is not unique, we all have our crosses to bear and our battles to overcome, but it is in sharing our story and troubles that we find out we are not on our own and yes, other people have also gone through their own hardships. But if we keep it all inside and don't communicate and continue to live within the pages of our own story, we will never know that we are part of a community, be it family, friends or even strangers and that we never need to battle on our own.

My need for independence or what I thought, were traits I brought with me into all my relationships, be it with partners and children alike. It was so ingrained in me that these traits have guiltily been passed down to my own children, especially my daughter. I not only lived and breathed it, but unconsciously almost had to prove a point that I didn't need anyone. I could do it all on my own, but in doing that, I was also pushing people away from me.

The biggest lesson I learnt, was that being independent doesn't mean you can't depend on people!

Now at 56 and recently retrenched from a 22-year career in the finance sector, I was forced to step out of my comfort zone and decide on a future I had no idea about. But the other side of that was, I also now had a freedom never availed to me before.

I am finally allowing myself to surrender and not have an outcome of what my life should look like. I am now in a place where I can recreate my future. So what is that going to look like? I don't quite know, but for the first time, I'm neither scared nor worried. I trust and know that the Universe (God) will show me the way and bring me the opportunities that are right for me. It is giving me the time to explore, time to allow my inner child the freedom and creativity it has been searching for such a long time.

Time to just Be and to be Me, whoever that may be.

I am now ready to receive and live the life I was always meant to.

As I hear the waves gently caressing the foreshore again, I am reminded of a life that is no longer mine.

It is now time to heal and ponder on what life was like, but above all smile, with gratitude in my heart, because I have come full circle and survived and so will you, my young Christine! Xx

Jump in Puddles: Releasing My Inner Child

Diane Psaila

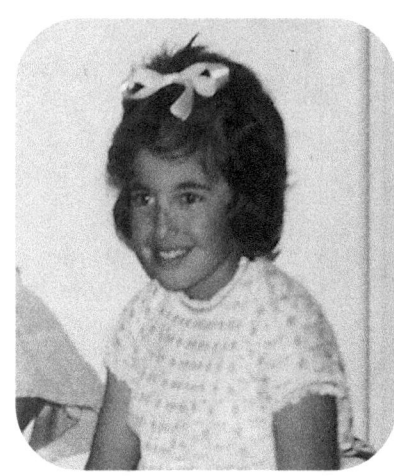 

Live your life like free-flowing energy as nothing compares to the warm, fuzzy feeling of beautiful moments without inhibitions.

Diane Psaila

It's raining!
The loud raindrops sound like corn popping as they hit the classroom roof.
Pop, pop, pop.
Slow at first, but the spaces between them are shorter now.
Yay, the home bell!
My grade five teacher reminds us to collect our test papers on the way out and to be careful going home.
We love our teacher because she is so nice to us.
We have merit awards for our good work.
Our work is only sometimes bad.
But she smiles and says, 'Next time we will try harder.'
We like to make her happy.
My blue raincoat is in my bag.
It's good that Mummy says to keep it in there just in case, but it hasn't rained for a long time.
I put it on and tuck my hair in the hood.
My sister meets me at our after-school spot.
She has her blue raincoat on too.
We walk fast steps along the footpath heading to home.
Big raindrops are hitting our hooded heads after sliding off the tree branches.
I love the smell of rain.

'It's just water,' I am told, 'It doesn't smell like anything,' but I guess their noses must be blocked.
Wet bark and dirt, yes, that's it.
The footpath looks grey today with shinny shapes instead of the freckled white ribbon all the way home.
Puddles are getting bigger and bigger, and it's hard to not step in them.
But I really want to.

That memory comes to mind now as I turn to the sound of a thunderclap. From my balcony early this morning I can see ominous dark storm clouds that are approaching from the West. The heavens open up, and the welcome rain hits the struggling earth to quench a deep thirst after months of drought; the earthy scent of steamy gratitude fills my nostrils.

The vivid sensation of free-flowing energy is exhilarating and takes me back to a time of childhood fun; innocent and carefree. At some point, it all seemed to have changed, where youth ended and the seriousness of acting like a grown-up took its place; a free spirit swamped by a series of conditions and cautions.

Bridging the gap between youth and adulthood has a sense of urgency, like an adrenalin of curiosity, a need to understand and find reason to decipher the mixed messages to find my unique purpose in life.

It's more than simply waking to the concept that I am who I am because it's how I want to be. Inbred influences, good and bad, have impacted how I think and react and how I live. It's a long road of discovery that I am still walking on and finding myself more open to surprise encounters and the courage to take up opportunities that are nurturing my passions.

When you think about it, from the moment we are born, we are open to learning. It's all-absorbing, like a dry sponge sitting in a pool of water on the kitchen bench, inheriting the manifest of knowledge and growth. It becomes a familiar environment, a creation of associations and a fundamental basis to our core, a footprint design on how we think, what we say and how we act.

From a young age I came to know that a simple 'yes' and 'no' are loaded statements dependant on the context in which they are said, who said it, and of course, body speak, which is a form of language all its own that can speak volumes. Imagine a child who is about to grab at a potted plant. The combination of a resounding 'no,' the parent's stern expression and wagging finger sends a clear warning message to the young mind to stop.

Social status seemed to matter a lot too and reminders that we were 'wogs' meant that we were often victims of ridicule and considered as those from the margins of society. Delicious and sometimes smelly 'wog' school lunches, combined with our not so perfect English language, brought about unwanted attention from our Anglo-Saxon peers. It was, still is today, perplexing to see people transform depending on who they were speaking to. It created an inferiority complex and a nervous expectation of unfair treatment, but on the flip side, it exposed gifts of awareness, a heightened emotional intelligence and particularly a greater connection with nature.

Nature's playground – an escapism that is real and without prejudice.

As a child, I loved to take notice of Nature with all its brilliance of contrasting outlooks, seasons, colours and shapes. It was a delight for me and still is. There is something truly magical about its energy; its extremes a timely reminder to put it all in perspective; our dependency for survival.

It was exhilarating to chase after the fairies (dandelions) and finding a 'wish' seed in the centre. We would solemnly think for a moment before making a wish at the same time as throwing the seed in the air. My wish was always for a special dog to call my own. There were the daisy chains too; the stem was pierced towards the bottom to feed through another daisy. With a great sense of triumph we fashioned them into long loops worn around our necks, a mix of white and yellow with brown centres against the green stems.

Those vivid memories bring on a smile and stir feelings of delightful innocence and warmth. Imagine a helicopter view. Groups of friends dotted around the oval, sitting, chatting and working at their daisy chains. Some would get up and run, pigtails swinging from side to side, the daisy chains bobbing up and down.

It's a reminder to strive in making that deep feeling of euphoria a repeated habit all through life. Setting out with a vision and taking the steps in making it real.

The awareness and connection to nature has become an antidote, a go-to place when life becomes too much of a muddle, when others' toxic behaviour threatens to invade my authenticity.

It's nice to enjoy that sense of freedom of just being me, without inhibitions, to feel safe and worthy of my existence and to express myself wholeheartedly in the company of like-minded people.

Identity crisis.

What happens as we grow? Why do some take on a distorted view of acceptable behaviour?

I have realised as I age that, 'keeping up appearances' or maintaining a 'camouflage', in conforming to the demands of society whether it is self-imposed or otherwise, takes great discipline and energy, especially if it is far removed from my authentic core. The transformation can stem from a multitude of reasons and responsibilities reliant on what 'hat' you are wearing and your intended audience. It's all good to establish a set of guidelines to co-exist and function as a team to achieve common objectives. However, to adopt an egotistical approach and achieve goals by ill-gotten methods such as discrediting others' potential to protect your own, is a recipe in creating disharmony and dysfunction.

Power and greed, hand in hand, fuelling more of the same.

It has a detrimental effect on those in their path, often powerless to take a stand with the lack of support or perhaps the courage to right a wrong to stop repeated inflictions.

I am the eldest, my sister following two years later and my brother arriving four years after her.

Grade three was a serious year at school. Our teacher was very strict, and a feather duster wasn't as airy-fairy as it sounds, and the dustpan brush wasn't made of plastic in those days, rather a solid, well-crafted piece of timber that fit snugly when gripped. Well, let's just say, they were, more often than not, used otherwise than for what they were intended. If we dared to say or do anything contradictory to the law of the classroom, there was a consequence that was promptly followed through and accompanied by a satisfied look of glee.

Our punishments did not fit our petty crimes, and many of us fell victim, clenching our jaws, our eyes stinging, holding back tears, as we bravely held out our reluctant little palms. We were frightened, and even then, we knew it was cruel and unjust, but there wasn't anything we could do, and we didn't dare say anything to our parents either as we must have been naughty to get into trouble. It was how it was and, in many ways, it toughened our endurance and adaptability to situations later in life.

'Daddy we don't have school today.'

'We didn't know about it?'

'You nearly forgot last time, remember?'

Daddy goes to our red telephone in the hallway.

I hear him say the lady's name who takes care of our brother when Mummy works.

Daddy goes to work at night time, but sometimes he has to go early.

He comes back and makes our breakfast.

I feel funny in my tummy, but it slowly goes away.

My sister is quiet.

She eats her breakfast, and I can see her looking at me without turning her head.

Daddy opens the kitchen venetian blinds that look out onto the street.

Oh, oh! I see it too!

There are school children walking past.

My funny tummy is back again.

Daddy looks at me and is very angry.

'Why did you say you don't have to go to school today?' he demands.

I start to cry and in big gulps, say, 'I didn't do all my homework.'

Daddy tells us to get dressed quickly, and before long we are standing in the school office.

The teacher comes to talk to Daddy.

She is smiling and looks different when she is talking to him.

Daddy tells us to be good and goes home.

Fight or flight. The primal instinct of survival.

I achieved high grades for my writing, spelling and math. Does the intense fear of failure and its consequence develop a distorted view of acceptable behavioural patterns to ensure success?

Was the teacher doing the same?

What would I say to that little girl now?

I would say that through fear of consequence, it took great courage to take *flight* and it was a *fight* in silent protest of treatment that was unjust.

The age of reform – open communication is key.

As I straightened my eldest son's shirt, proudly looking down as his handsome face full of excitement to head off to his first day in the classroom, I hugged him tightly and blurted out a few last-minute instructions, 'Have fun and make sure you listen to your teacher.'

In the week before, I had already talked about being respectful of people, not to bully or hit anyone if they make you mad, and that no-one should do that to him and to let me know if something is bothering him.

I was being overprotective, I know, however, it was peace of mind for me. The anger and pain of physical and psychological injuries being inflicted on the vulnerable for petty or imagined crimes came to the surface. It's a different world now from that eventful year at primary school and that year did not define my whole experience, however it left an imprint on my mind that is attached to strong emotion. You never forget it.

Everyone has the right to feel safe.

Back then, our parents barely interacted with the teachers as it was just not done. There wasn't the convenience of communication technologies allowing greater transparency, knowledge and involvement that we have come to take for granted in our lifestyles nowadays. They worked long hours, and the language barrier would have been a factor; therefore, they were oblivious of discipline taken to extremes. When the sealed report card came home, it told them everything they needed to know, and luckily for me, it was good.

A bad experience can lead to greater growth.

I can't remember how it actually happened, but I know the blackboard was becoming more and more of a blur towards the end of grade 5 and I soon was very sick with a virus that invaded my body aggressively. I was absent from school for six weeks. Very weak and unable to get out of bed unassisted; the coughing and the phlegm felt like it was choking me. Mum and Dad would have me over an upturned kitchen chair tapping my back firmly to bring it up. It was exhausting for all of us, and it wasn't a pretty sight, but it did help. Mum would cry each time I was taken to the hospital for weekly injections; my arms resembling pin cushions.

My hair was cut very short so it would be easier to manage. I remember feeling ugly and looking like a boy and the bright blue cat-eye glasses just added to the insult. I wish I could reach out to my vulnerable younger self right now and say that image isn't everything; what is on the inside is all that matters.

When I was able to sit up and concentrate my sister would bring home school work. She was sad for me and also upset that false rumours were being circulated that I had hepatitis and children were told to keep away and not play with her and our brother in case they should get sick too. They were treated as outcasts; fear, driven by ignorance. It was awful, but that vivid experience has brought up the significant values of compassion and respect.

Mum and Dad did all they could to keep my mind active. Reading books was already a great passion and stamp collecting became a hobby too that I could do while I was recuperating. I was fascinated with the different images on the stamps, the sizes of them, their musty smell and the countries they represented.

It's great, as children, to open our minds beyond our everyday routines and the advice works well for adults too as it adds greater dimension to our way of thinking and an appreciation of cultural differences that can stir a curiosity to know more.

My sister would be sent on an errand to the school library to borrow related books. This preoccupation, I'm sure, aided my recovery, and I surfaced, with a state of mind ready to take on the world again.

For a child articulating words to feelings may be difficult; however the experience becomes an embedded memory of life's fragility. Moving forward from an episode at any stage in life does change your outlook, but it is an opportunity to acknowledge what was and to move forward positively.

When I returned to school, my grade five teacher was overjoyed to see me. Mum and Dad were told that I had integrated back into school life without any difficulty, and they were very pleased.

As for me, it was wonderful to see my friends again who gathered around with excitement and took delight in getting me up to speed with the schoolyard gossip. I was missed and the worried thoughts of looking like a boy, even with my new glasses, soon disappeared.

Fairy wishes do come true!

The TV series *Lassie* was a family favourite from the first time we started watching at the end of primary school and into secondary school, so you can imagine the thrill when Dad's boss and his wife asked that we have their Rough Collie over while they were on holidays. 'Lindy' looked identical to *Lassie*, the markings on her coat and her temperament too.

Lindy and I formed an immediate bond, and it broke my heart when the time came for Dad's boss to collect her after they came back from their holiday. I wanted to keep her. Adjusting back to when she wasn't at home was hard to do as she knew so many tricks and would keep up with me when I rode my bike. Days were long without Lindy around, but as the weeks and months went by, routines went back to how they were before.

I opened the gate and walked into the yard.
'Mum, Dad!'
'How come Lindy is back?'
Lindy is on a lead tied to the washing line, and when she sees me, she vigorously wags her tail.
I run to set her free, and we jump around and hug.
'Dad?'
'My boss bought an apartment, and they can't have a dog,' says Dad.
'Can we keep her?'
'Can we, please!'
'Yes, we can,' Dad says with a smile on his face.
I jump with happiness!

So, you see, never giving up hope and the virtue of patience goes a long way.

Lindy, where are you?

Years later, my brother and I rode our bikes up and down neighbouring streets, parks and schools calling for Lindy. She had been quieter than usual for the last few days, and now she had gone walk-a-bout and was missing. I was distraught. Where is she? I must find her. Neighbours and friends had looked out for her too. After a couple of days when I was starting to lose hope, in she limps, dirty and hungry, although she only managed to eat a nibble of food. I went with Dad to the vet. Lindy was sick; very sick. She had a growth on her neck. It was the hardest experience of my young life to say goodbye to my beloved Lindy. The grieving process changed me. I grew up.

Loss teaches you that nothing is forever. More so, the stronger the connection, the harder the struggle with adjusting to the loss, if ever. Writing this still brings tears to my eyes, but from this end, I was thrilled that all those fairy wishes for a dog paid off as the rewards of having that unique relationship is a memory that will last forever.

Sweet success; giddy with excitement.

It was rare for us, but sometimes we stopped in at the milk bar just down the road from our primary school with five cents in hand. We would point at the lollies through the big, bubble-shaped glass counter window that held rows of a blissful array of brightly coloured shaped lollies, some in wrappers and some without. I had always wondered why that was. It's not like they tasted extra special or anything like that, but it was fun unwrapping a *Milko* and stopping halfway and wrapping it up again to save some for later. The big decision was choosing what I wanted; *Humbugs, Musk Sticks* and *Bananas* were a given, and *Jaffas, Mates* and *Milk Bottles* usually weren't far behind. I will never forget scurrying out with the little white paper bag in hand and hurrying my sister and brother to get home in time to watch *Scooby-Doo*.

Why is the association of eating something sweet a parallel to feel-good moments? As children, the allure was just as much their shape and colour in addition to taste and how they made you feel after eating them. Marketers targeted their young clientele cleverly; however, we were repeatedly cautioned by our parents not to eat too much as it was like poison to our bodies and we would die. I think we were too young to understand the concept around moderation, so an impact statement involving death did the trick.

The effects of serotonin, the good mood brain chemical, brings about a calm to ease frustration and stress. Life can present overwhelming challenges; for me it was dealing with the pressures in maintaining a consistent balance and safe environment in nurturing care and growth for my three children. It was easy to reach out and indulge in a quick fix of non-healthy options as go-to comfort food to ease the feelings of threat. It does feel good for a time, however it led to uncomfortable weight gain which dampened my mood, and the cycle would start over again. It was like a stagnate existence; shoes stuck in a muddy puddle anchoring the ability to move forward.

A strong message to share and reinforce at any age is that we don't need to walk alone when the odds seem to be stacking up against us. Damaging habits only disguise underlying issues and will not resolve why we set on a course that is averse to positive growth in the first place.

Adopting a mindset of empowerment releases feelings of jubilation. Take control and act. Once the first step is taken, mastering the momentum becomes a series of determined steps in the right direction. To care for others, you must first care for yourself. It makes perfect sense.

Just as I reflect on messages to send to the younger version of myself, I can also learn from my youth. It is there within us; our core values. Create a safety shield, an environment of nourishment for the mind, embrace growth, learn from the wise and acknowledge that strengths and weaknesses are our right as a unique individual.

~~~~

The thunder and lightning show are fading now, but the rain is steadily saturating the garden and filling the rock pond. After a leave of absence for many months, it seems incredulous, however rejuvenation is visible already, almost as if life has been in suspension, waiting for this moment in time, an opportunity for reflection and renewal to take its rightful place.

A car slows in front of the house, and I see an arm extending from the driver's window.

Taking aim, the daily newspaper is thrown and lands in the garden.

The image reminds me of a story between two elderly gentlemen as they painstakingly sort through their work materials:

'Can't see today's young folk bothering with this work, eh Bill?'
'Was just saying to the Missus this morning about the paper being delivered as a drive-by; thrown from the car window!'
'Whatever happened to paperboys on pushbikes?'.

'No backbone this generation.'
'It's hard yakka that toughens boys into men.'
'No time then to cause trouble.'
'Too right Dave.'

Is that how today's younger generation are perceived?

Were we, in our youth, thought of in this way by our elders?

The generation gap – forming an understanding – why and how it matters.

Each generation grew up in a different set of living circumstances moulding them into what they consider is important as a benchmark to prevalent beliefs, influences from the effects of war times, traditional and cultural beliefs and the impacts of political agendas. The list goes on with the surge in technologies, accessibility to higher education, significance of social and materialistic gain, men and women stereotypes and equal opportunity.

Often a statement would surface on, 'How easy the young ones have it these days.'

That statement would set off animated discussions around the table with each generation advocating that when growing up, their lot had it the hardest.

Grandpa and Grandma: The Silent Generation or Traditionalists speak on memories of childhood:

'It was simple and fun; our inventive toys were made from bits and pieces around the home.'

'We were very young during WW2. Confusion, fear and running to the shelters when the warning sirens sounded of the approaching enemy planes became a way of life.'

'As the war raged on, our day to day supplies of food, clothing and other basic necessities were becoming hard to find. Nothing was ever wasted. Two worn bedsheets would be cut to make one. A woman's dress fashioned into girls' dresses and only one pair of shoes until they were worn out or handed down to a sibling when they didn't fit our growing feet anymore.'

'Survival during those unstable and dangerous times rendered us a resilient generation. Even from a young age, we came to know to never take anything for granted, and the expectation was for us to work hard at our chores in silence and we did just that.'

'We were barely adults when we immigrated to Australia. Nothing was gained unless it was earned, and we worked long, hard hours to pave the way to a better future. There wasn't plastic money like nowadays, which meant if we didn't have the money, we just went without.'

Generation Y jump in:

'It's a different world we live in now, but we have our pressures too.'

'Yes, we acknowledge that our grandparents experienced extremes that were life-changing but we can't be blamed for not feeling the same way as we weren't there. We have different threats in our society today that affects our everyday life.'

'We are living amidst the technology boom and, in many aspects, it has made life so much simpler, yet it has also imposed pressures in keeping up with it all. We are self-centred in how we view our priorities, and we are not shy to speak our mind; however it doesn't mean we are disrespectful and don't appreciate family and home. It's a competitive world out there, and materialistic wealth is important to us, and this often means we are expected to be on call 24/7 with work and life.'

I throw in my viewpoint: Generation X:

'My adolescent memories are of traditional family values, of completing chores around the home before any play was allowed, working hard at school to secure a well-paying job and the importance to save money.'

'The family unit was a focus on the love and pride of home and routine, of family outings after Sunday mass and camping holidays away by the sea or to the country at Easter and Christmas. I remember the race to answer the ring of the red telephone sitting on its own hallway stand and how we sat in awe when the lounge room television went from black and white to colour.'

'We were caught in the middle when we got to our teens, of doing what was expected of us and the need for freedom to explore our way in the world. A deviation to our parents' way of thinking meant there was conflict and feelings would surface of suppression; our natural right threatened. Leaving home meant you were getting married and not before as it mattered what the relatives thought and reputation was everything.'

'Becoming a mother has deepened my understanding of love and the vested responsibility to raise a family'.

I think of those strict, awkward years from my teens to adulthood and sometimes wish it had been different, until one night at a family Christmas celebration at a Mt Buller lodge:

Christmas 2003. Summer. Family.

The Mt Buller lodge, after a Winter season abuzz with skiers and snow-covered mounts, had an outlook of dense, green Eucalypt trees. The sounds of cackling kookaburras accompanied the striking sights of golden sunrises and crimson sunsets. The high altitude caused shortness of breath when power walking with my sister-in-law, and we carried on in silence. We filled our nostrils with the crisp air filled with the fresh scent of Eucalypts, and below the embankment, we heard the soothing sounds of fresh water running down gullies. Good for the soul.

It set the scene.

Mum and my aunty had one of their sisters visiting from Malta. Siblings and cousins seated opposite them asked about the old days and the circumstances surrounding their mother's death at the young age of

40 and what happened then to the four sisters as they had lost their father at age 36.

What came then has completed the pieces of the puzzle. The three sisters' haunting memories of being orphaned at a young age, not knowing what was to happen to them next, brought on a recount of anguish of the cruel twist of fate. I had never heard my mum talk openly like that before and it looked like they were sharing their feelings for the first time. My cousin went to embrace her mum and my sister-in-law ran for the tissue box and made cups of tea.

It was a sad and emotional sight, however, my sister, brother and I needed to see that. Children can't appreciate the bigger picture, and it all makes sense now. The certain reactions by my parents when we were young, the overstated protectiveness and the need to keep the family unit intact.

It was a lesson of the need to understand and to rewrite a childhood memory.

Expectations and attitudes differ between the generations, therefore understanding the why and how can aid in bridging the gap, creating a harmonious environment and avoiding getting caught up in a generational crossfire.

This can be at any age; as a daughter or son, as a parent, and functioning as a go-between one and the other. Growth is wisdom; an opportunity to challenge your best and in turn, help others to do the same.

~~~~

The rain eases and streaks of golden sunlight pierce the clouds brightening the grey morning.

It has a surreal effect.

The droplets of rain are glistening like jewels; Nature's blessing.

I take this opportunity to walk down to collect the newspaper.

There are puddles in my path.

I smile.

Jump in puddles, is a metaphor.
Take the risk to explore what's possible.
Push past those inhibitions that hold you back.
Past those who say you can't.
Say no when it isn't right.
Growth is all the lessons of yesteryears.
Of understanding the depth of people.
Their part in this present you are living.
You are here and now.
Live that exhilaration that is life.
'Release my inner child,' I tell myself.'

Dreams Can Come True

Gail Conley

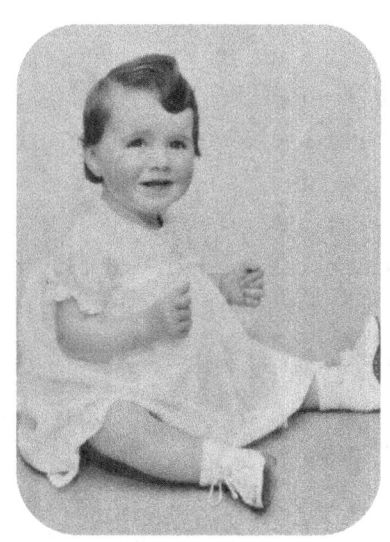 

Being positive in life is all that matters.
The universe does the rest.

Gail Conley

A Message To Your Younger Self

Facing death, the miracle of life and learning to rise above when faced with family tragedy.

Guardian Angels are holding your hand through the good, bad and in between – keeping you safe, giving you courage and sometimes saving your life.

It was a normal day, like any other in my three-year-old life. My brother and his friend were playing in the backyard pool. I was too little to go swimming without an adult present, so I just watched them. They were playing a game of dead man floating. They floated face-first on the water holding their breath for as long as they could. The one that held their breath the longest, won.

They lay floating for a while, then jumped up splashing, gasping for a breath, then laughing. This went on for a while until they are sick of being in the pool and decided to go down the shop for lollies. They left me alone at the pool. Eight-year-olds do not think of the implications of this action. Mum had no idea they had left me, and I was alone.

The water looked very inviting, and I had just seen my brother and his friend having so much fun. I jumped in the pool but I couldn't swim or hold myself above the water. I sank to the bottom of the pool out of breath and clinically dead.

The neighbour Wendy heard a loud scream and a large crack. When she ran outside, she found Mum with lifeless me in her arms. Lucky for me Aunty Wendy had read about how to administer mouth to mouth resuscitation in the Herald Sun only days earlier. She put her learning into practice and low and behold she saved my life. I am lucky and so grateful to her for the gift of life I received that day. Mum would not leave me alone in the bathtub until I was a teenager due to her fears of me drowning again.

My memories of this event are of seeing a bright light like the sun. It could have been the sun. It could have been Divine intervention. Then I saw Aunty Wendy's smiling face. I was then rushed off to the doctor to check if I was okay.

The news got out, and the Herald-Sun newspaper came to take photos and write our special story.

GAIL O'KEEFE, 3, gave Mrs Wendy Donnelly a very special kiss last night

For earlier in the day. Mrs Donnelly saved Gail's life...with a kiss.

When the Sun published the 'kiss of life' method of

> lifesaving last month, Mrs Donnelly, of Pecham Street, Glenroy learnt it off by heart. Yesterday she was glad that she had done so.
>
> Mrs Donnelly said she could hear screams from the backyard of a neighbour, Mrs Phyllis O'Keefe. 'I rushed outside and saw Mrs O'Keefe clutching Gail in her arms,' Mrs Donnelly said.
>
> Mrs O'Keefe had found Gail lying face down in their backyard swimming pool. Gail was not breathing. 'I laid her on the ground and began to apply mouth to mouth,' Mrs Donnelly said. 'I've no idea how long it was before she started to breathe again. If I had not seen the Sun's article I wouldn't have been able to do it.'
>
> Last night Gail, unharmed after her ordeal was resting at home.
>
> *Article and picture from Herald Sun Newspaper 1971.*

Aunty Wendy took me into their pool the next day to make sure I was not in fear of water after the ordeal. All was well, I was okay, but we never had a swimming pool again.

In 2016 we had a reunion of all the neighbours from Pecham Street, Glenroy, where I grew up. I met up again with Aunty Wendy. It was 46 years after she had saved my life. I hugged her and whispered, 'Thank you so much for saving my life.' She tells me that she always wondered how I would be considering how long I was clinically dead. She said her children thought that I was a black dog she was holding in her arms that day.

I felt so glad that I was able to thank her before she passed. It was something I always wanted to do. It gave me closure to hear her recount the events of that day and answer the questions I had in my mind about how it all had happened.

As a child, you live with your head in the clouds, a free spirit not paying attention to the world around you. There were many other occasions when my brother saved me. There was the time I nearly was run over by a car and the time the Ferris Wheel at the Royal Melbourne Show nearly crushed me.

A significant memory was the time when I was singing out loud on the way home from school, and I swallowed a bee. I was choking and my throat was swelling. I grabbed my brother's arm and managed to gasp, 'I can't breathe.' My brother threw me over his shoulder and ran home.

Luckily again, Aunty Wendy came to my aid, taking me in her car to the doctor. My mum did not have a licence and Dad was not home. The doctor removed the sting and said I was lucky my brother rushed me home as I could have died from my throat swelling from a bee sting. In these cases, my brother was my saviour.

My brother has had his own scrapes with death by way of serious car accidents. When he was 13, he took a road trip with his mates. The driver lost control and the car veered off the round and rolled sixteen times. There were seven in the car and not all the passengers had seatbelts on, and as a result they were thrown out of the vehicle. Tragically, two of his friends died that day, and the other passengers all sustained minor injuries. My brother was in hospital in a coma for two weeks. He had a broken ankle and a lot of bruising and lacerations. In the same year, he was the passenger in a head-on accident and sustained a broken collarbone.

Years later, in his thirties, my brother flew out the back of a Suzuki Vitara soft top vehicle. He was not wearing a seatbelt. He hit the bitumen at 60 km per hour and sustained very serious injuries to his knee with gravel embedded in his skin. He spent two weeks in hospital with daily cleaning and bandaging of his wounds.

A few years later he wrapped his car around a tree and walked away with a broken rib. And if that was not enough, he was recently working on the Bunyip State fires driving a grader clearing firebreaks. The wind turned and the fire came back on him. He could smell the hairs on his arms burning and was sure his time was up. Luckily for him, the CFA fire crew saw what was happening and put out the flames under the grader.

I often tell him he is lucky, and he has guardian angels looking after him. He disagrees saying, 'I am not lucky, how can you say that considering all of the things that have happened to me.' I beg to differ. He still has his life and he is still here to tell the tales.

From very young I learned about death and loss. My grandmother on Mum's side and my room-mate left me when I was only eight. This was my first experience of death, and I found it very hard as she was like a best friend to me. I could not figure out how she could just be gone like that. She has become my guiding angel, and I know she has been with me on many occasions during my life providing comfort.

My grandmother on Dad's side passed when I was thirteen. She had pancreatic cancer, and it was heartbreaking watching her shrink into a tiny sick old lady. She was such a bright spark and laughed often. She gave the best hugs goodbye which always included a little change for lollies.

Then age nineteen, I had just moved out with my future husband Brett, when Mum was admitted to hospital and diagnosed with bowel cancer. They operated, but cancer had taken over her liver, and there was no hope for her. Three weeks later on Boxing Day, Mum left us. I was with her when she died along with her sister and my sister. The strangest thing was that the night before I had been hearing her calling me and I knew I had to be with her when she passed. She often lets me know she is with me through songs playing over the radio, most commonly Abba's *Dancing Queen*.

Dad came to live with Brett and me after selling the family home. We were happy together moving to our first home in Kinglake. Dad spent his time with us and his home in Stratford that Nana had left him. My brother and his family were living there, so Dad got to see him and the grandkids when he visited. Unfortunately, just four years after we lost Mum, Dad was diagnosed with bowel cancer. They operated, and he has a colostomy bag until they could operate to re-join the bowel that had been removed.

Brett and I getting married was one of the proudest days of Dad's life. I will never forget how wonderful it was seeing Dad so happy at our wedding and having a ball. Soon after our wedding, Dad had the second operation to re-join the bowel, but cancer had spread to his liver, and he was only with us for another seven months. I helped my brother care for Dad until the end, travelling between Kinglake and Stratford. It was truly heartbreaking for us to see Dad shrink and lose all his lust for life. Brett was my rock during this time, but he was hurting too as they were close.

My mother-in-law and father-in-law were always there for me offering love, wisdom and advice. Brett and I were together from quite a young age, so they became my mum and dad number 2. Mum would always write on my cards, 'Love Always Mum and Dad No. 2'. When we lost Brett's mum from dementia and his dad seven months later, it was such a tragedy for my husband and his siblings. They had not faced loss like this. But they were very strong and the way they all handled the situation was a true credit to them.

His mum and dad showed such love and courage. I believe they have been looking over us, and it was more than fate that we found our wonderful paradise home. We always chatted with Mum and Dad number 2 about living on a farm and having a house on the hill. I was astonished as we drove past our home to be. When we finally had the opportunity to buy our forever place, it was just as we had imagined, a farm with a house on the hill. You cannot make this stuff up. Everything fell into place.

What I have learned about life is that you never know what happens next despite how much you think you have things under control. Tragedy can strike anybody, anywhere and it has no discrimination. It is how we deal with the situations that arise that is the important thing.

We can rise above the bad and look forward to living one day at a time. Give yourself time to heal and release. Seek help if need be. Be grateful, be loving and show kindness, especially to those in need. Try to see the best in everyone and everything. And most importantly, be happy, laugh a lot and seek joy in your life. And if you believe as I do, be grateful to our angels and guides for showing the way through the darkness to the light.

Love, faith, hope and having patience.

Dreams come true. I believe that when we apply love, faith, hope and have patience, the universe holds this space in time for us, and everything will be revealed.

It was the first day of Technical School, and I was walking through the corridor of the science building looking for my classroom. I saw this good looking spunk of a boy. He had blonde, curly hair and blue eyes. He looked like Bow Duke, my idol from The *Dukes of Hazzard,* my favourite television show. I knew right then that he would be the one I would want to be with my entire life.

In a matter of days, I had asked around and knew his name, and luckily for me, my brother's girlfriend knew him. She had gone out with his brother and said she would organise for us to meet. I was so excited and could not wait. So I was sitting at the school's Trade Block and coming towards me were my brother's girlfriend with Brett Conley. She introduced us, and he ran away. He was very shy, so our first meeting did not go very well. I thought he didn't like me, so I didn't pursue him. I did watch him all that year hanging around with his friends at their regular spot. The next year I looked out for him, but he had left school. I was sad as I thought I wouldn't get the opportunity to see him again.

My girlfriend and I were hanging out in her bedroom as we often did. We were writing songs and pretending we were rock goddesses. We chatted about boys and asked each other all the boys we knew and who would we like to go out with. I said Brett Conley of course, and she tells me who she liked. Well, it so happened that I could set her up with the guy she picked and he tells me he can set me up with Brett. OMG, I was so excited and hopeful that we would get together.

We had our first date about eighteen months after I had set eyes on him and to my surprise, he did not remember me or that he had run away from me at our first meeting. From that night, the 8th August 1981 until now, I have been together with my soulmate.

Patience, love, hope and faith brought us together. The universe had the plan and time caught up with it. I am forever grateful for this man, the love of my life, a great father, my rock and never-ending source of laughter. We shall be happy forever as dreams do come true when you wish hard enough.

Another truly fortunate event in my life was the job I applied for and ended up working at for twenty-nine years. I first started working in factories when I left school at the end of year 10. The reason for leaving school was I wanted my independence and money. As the years went by, I realised that I had made a mistake. While I had my independence, I was not challenged by the work. Anyone can do the repetitive process work I was doing, and it was boring. I wanted something more. I wanted to help people if I could. I wanted job satisfaction.

I had heard about traineeships being offered and went to the employment agency, but they claimed they did not know anything about them. I knew they were wrong and wondered how I could get a traineeship. I went to a place called Youth Projects who offered me a course in administration. Great! I could do this course and wait for the traineeships to commence. That is what I did. I finished my course, and the staff at Youth Projects helped me access the forms to apply for the traineeship.

I applied for the Broadmeadows, Kensington and Flemington Community Health Centres. I was turned down by Broadmeadows as they wanted someone with more experience and year 11 as a prerequisite. I attended the interview for Kensington and Flemington together. I told them of my experience at Broadmeadows and felt it was unfair. I told them of my efforts to get to that point, going back to school and studying the course in administration. I admitted that I didn't have a great deal of office experience but that I was truly willing to learn. I wanted to work at a place where I could help people, especially those less fortunate.

The interview was very successful, and I had my choice of Flemington or Kensington to do my traineeship. I chose Flemington as I was told I would learn more with the various tasks on reception. I loved this job, and at the end of the traineeship, I was so sad I had to go. They tried hard to get funding for me to stay but to no avail. I was offered a job in head office Community Services. I took it reluctantly hoping I could get back to Flemington. To my surprise, Flemington did a restructure and offered me a full-time receptionist position a few months later. I was over the moon and back where I belonged.

Over the next 29 years, I moved from reception to administration officer to HR/Payroll Officer to Senior Payroll Manager. It was a wonderful place to work; looking after the staff who looked after the community. I was witness to much hardship, triumph and change in the community health sector over the years. I left because the organisation became too big and I felt I no longer had anything to offer. I pursued my new dream of helping people through tarot/oracle reading and energy healing. My business, *Chakra Angel Oracle,* began.

What I have learned about life is that if you dream hard enough and are determined to stay focused, you can eventually see a dream come true. The universe has the plan, and you have to apply your love, your faith, your hope and be patient. Things will work out in most instances. If things don't work out as intended, you will have an important lesson. Some of our biggest mistakes are our biggest lessons.

Pay it forward.

What goes around, comes around. Good karma comes from good deeds and sacrifices.

Throughout my life, I have tried to be the best person I could be. I married my soul mate, and we had two beautiful boys who became gentlemen we could be proud of. My husband and I always worked hard to give our family a good start. We have helped our family in times of need. I worked in the community sector as I thought I could help others and make a difference. I always made sure I did whatever I could to help the clients and staff feel they were comfortable and listened to. I am kind, honest and helpful. I am not afraid to stand up for those who need a voice either.

Most of my life I have been a carer for my sister who needed a voice as she negotiated the mental health system. There were times where she needed me to make sure they looked after all her needs, both physically and mentally. We provided accommodation for my brother and his two boys for several years while they worked nearby on the Craigieburn Bypass.

Our home has been a haven for our sons' friends at times when they needed a place to stay. You can count on Brett and I to be there for our family and friends. We love animals great and small and have taken care of dogs, lizards, birds, cats, guinea pigs, chickens, fish, ferrets, snakes and even Mexican Walking fish. Most came to us as pets and others as rescues.

I believe karma has afforded me a vision of something new. It was a vision of a place that had a beautiful home with large windows that looked over a lake. Wow! The universe was giving me a present. My friend and soul sister who is a psychic medium told me the house was on a lake. I thought it must be in Lakes Entrance, so I proceeded to look at places around that area. I did not know when I would be there, but I was going to follow this vision and do what I could to be there.

We sold our family home of 22 years within three weeks of it being on the market and arranged to have a 12-month settlement. We ticked off our first step towards paradise and had six months to look for the place that was in my vision. We had a fair idea of the area we wanted to live in but were looking for a place with 100 or so acres. They were not many places in our search area with our requirements.

I was talking to my guides and asking them, 'You have given me this vision, and we have been looking, when are we going to find the place you are showing me?' I heard back from them that the place is waiting for me but that I just hadn't been there yet. I kept looking, and another clairvoyant friend advised me that I would find my dream home in May.

It came to the beginning of May, and nothing was promising. I was feeling a little frustrated and impatient. But I kept faith in knowing that my guides had given me this vision and there was a plan.

Towards the end of May, my brother's girlfriend told us about a place that we might like, but the price was more than we had budgeted. I made an appointment to view it nevertheless.

OMG, the place was everything I wanted and more. This was the home in my vision. I was standing looking out of the large windows towards the lake. The place is on Lake Victoria near Bairnsdale. I went numb and my hands started buzzing with energy. I had set a crystal grid with a friend to help me know when and if this home was the one. My brother and husband walked around inspecting the property and Brett fell in love with this place too.

We put in a bid and there was another person bidding as well. I told the real estate agent we would bid the asking price with no finance required as I knew the other bidders would buy subject to finance. The only stipulation was that we needed a six-month settlement. The agent went back to the owners and said they would let us know the next day if we were successful.

The next morning the agent called and congratulated us advising that we were the successful bidders and the home was ours. We were very happy and this new home was everything we could wish for and more. Thank you guides and universe for this wonderful new start.

I am grateful for this chance to pay it forward. I know my purpose is continuing to help people wherever I can. I am currently studying for my Diploma in Community Services and will be looking for part-time employment in the community sector.

I will continue to run my business *Chakra Angel Oracle* offering readings and energy healing to the public in my Angel and Healing Rooms. If I can help people find their way on this journey of life then I am fulfilling my mission.

I give thanks for the vision that was divinely given to me as a reward. I believe that it was good karma for good deeds and sacrifices throughout our lives.

The universe has paid it forward. My life has a purpose and I am ready for whatever comes to us as we build our new life here in Paradise on Lake Victoria, ready to pay it forward to others.

How $6 Changed My Life

Suzanne Therese Costello

Always consider the consequences of your choices, take the advice of others, and choose what will make you happy long term.

Suzanne Therese Costello

A Message To Your Younger Self

Dearest Zanny

There are many pivotal moments and key decision points in life, but you weren't to know that one of yours would be the importance of $6 and what you would give up for it. The past cannot be changed, but it's good to look back and learn from it.

The seventies were such simpler times, and there is no denying that people lived much less frenetic lives than we do now. In 1970 you left your home in Ararat where the family had been living since January 1968. You had finished your secondary schooling by scraping a reasonable pass in your Matriculation exams at Marian College Ararat. That was when the next stage of your life began, when you had to stand on your own two feet and go out into the world. Well, maybe not quite the world but to Melbourne to study. Before I remind you of that, you must look back a little to give the decision that would change your life, context.

You had been a bright student throughout your school days, but in 1968 you were suddenly at a co-educational convent run by the Brigidine Sisters. This proved to be such a distraction as for the first time since primary school, there were those creatures we call boys in the room. You were very soon enamoured of one of them, and you couldn't concentrate as much as you should have; you daydreamed through classes hardly hearing a word that was said.

Lovestruck teenagers must have been a real challenge for the nuns. It was probably very obvious to all within a country mile that you were totally smitten with Michael.

He returned your sly glances, and you would sidle up to wherever he was and try and sit just that bit closer than how teenage classmates should have sat. By August of that year when you were turning 16, Michael asked if you would go to a 21st birthday party with him. Of course, you would. Your Mum made you a new minidress and Michael organised for his parents to pick you up.

You probably won't remember too much of the night, but you were with Michael and that was enough excitement for any young girl. After that one date he didn't ask you out again, and you were a bit crushed.

The Christmas school holidays in the late '60s were six-week breaks, and summer fun was pretty much hanging around at the local swimming pool with all the other kids from your school and the kids from the High School as well. Nobody had pools in their backyards back then or at least none of the kids you knew did.

A Message To Your Younger Self

Twelve months earlier when you had arrived in the hot, dry, dusty town, your Mum was still unpacking when she said to you, 'Take your sisters to the pool to cool off and hopefully you will meet some kids from your new schools.' She was right.

On the first or second day there, you noticed two girls about your age checking you out. They eventually sauntered over and asked you if you were new in town. Many questions later it was established that you would all be in Form 5 at the convent. The chattier one of the two said, 'Stick with us, and we will look out for you.'

You saw Carmel and Peggy a few times at the pool before school began. Years down the track you will still be friends with Carmel, and hers is one of the birthday emails you still receive every August 13th. Sadly, we lost the lovely Peggy many years ago to cancer; she was the first of your peers to check out young.

But back to 1968. As it was a small school you were all together in one large classroom for most of the main classes and the timetable was worked out so that the people studying typing and shorthand would leave the classroom and go off to the typing room. Science subjects were held in a special room as well, and there might have been a few others like a music room and possibly an art room. You didn't do either subject so you mostly stayed in the main classroom.

Sport was compulsory, and you played tennis and netball, neither very well I might add. Whilst you were quite tall, you were very uncoordinated and often fell over especially when playing netball. You were featured in the local paper though one week at the netball courts. The photographer had snapped a great shot when both your feet were off the ground and your pigtails were flying upwards in the air. Being the collector of ephemera that you have always been, I am sure you will have that picture filed away to one day show your grandchildren.

One of your classmates, a girl called Marie, quickly became your friend. She was a boarder from a large Irish Catholic family. Her parents had decided to send their children off to boarding schools all over the Western District. As Marie was one of 12 children, it was possibly considered a way of the children finding themselves.

Sometime during 1968, you noticed that Marie had been hanging on Michael's every word just as you were. I remember how she leant in one day and said, 'I really like Michael. He is cute.'

Zanny, I am so proud of you that you didn't act like a jealous teenager often does. That would have been a sad thing to happen, and you would have regretted losing Marie's friendship over a boy.

That summer of 1968-69 was a very hot dry time, and unfortunately, there were very bad fires all over Victoria. A very nasty fire raged around the edges of Ararat for a few days covering the sky in a shroud of smoke, the ashes even rained down on your Mum's washing line which meant she had to start the process again. One very scary day the fires were just across the other side of the cemetery only a block away from your house, and your granny and mother stayed at the house with the garden hose at the ready.

You, being the eldest, were sent with your four siblings up to the oval at the top of the street. You kept a watchful eye on the sky and which way the wind was blowing. Finally, late in the evening, the wind had changed and the crisis was averted. You were all tired and hot as you trudged down Fay St to that house that held all your family's belongings. You could finally relax.

Michael and his friend Andrew had been doing some hay carting out on a farm during the holidays, and they were on the back of a truck fighting fires when it rolled. They were both injured in the accident and taken to the Ararat Hospital. The news of the accident spread quickly around the town. Your Mum was the one who encouraged you to go to visit Michael, 'Here, have 60 cents to buy him a block of chocolate at Kink's Milk Bar on the way to the hospital.' You didn't need much encouragement.

He was pleased to see you, and you stayed a little longer than you probably thought you would. Remember you had only been out together once, but as school friends, you had seen him every day so there was a lot to chat about.

The holidays were soon over, and school began again. It was your final year, Form 6 or Matriculation as it was called. A good result in the exams would mean that you could get into a course of Teacher Training at a variety of institutions around the state. By the middle of that year, you and Michael were going steady. It sounds such a quaint, old-fashioned term but in 1969 it had replaced an even quainter one that most probably was used by your parents. They would have said they were courting in their day.

The successful applicants into Teacher Training were offered Studentships by the Government. They also provided hostels for country students to live in. It was a cheaper way of obtaining a qualification than by going to university and paying the fees upfront – the only people who could afford that were the sons and daughters of wealthy pastoralists and professionals.

You, a daughter of a railwayman, were not going to get an education unless the government assisted you in a major way. Michael was planning on going to Melbourne too, to study interior design at RMIT. It sounded like a good plan, and he was going to board with his older brother and sister-in-law, who by chance happened to live almost around the corner from the Secondary Teachers Hostel in Orrong Rd Armadale where you would be living if you passed the exams.

Congratulations Zanny, you did pass, not brilliantly, but well enough to get the coveted Studentship and to be able to enrol at Melbourne University's Secondary Teachers College. You thought that was what you wanted but how could you know that in less than a year you would throw away this opportunity for a measly $6 a week.

There was a lot to be done before you were going off to the big smoke. Your mother was a brilliant seamstress who had always made your clothes. She was very talented, and with any fabric she could acquire, would whip up a mini dress in a couple of hours on her Singer sewing machine. She made you a few new dresses and had scrimped and saved to be able to send you off with nice new underclothes, new shoes and all the usual things girls of seventeen needed.

Her gift to you as you left home was a beautiful mohair travel rug. You knew how handy that would be on all the trips up and down on the train that you would make. In those days the trains were not heated or cooled like today's trains and even on the weekends when you managed to get a lift back to Ararat with Barry Price the Collingwood footballer, his car was draughty in the back seat. Barry's parents lived around the corner from your parents and he was kind enough to give you, a poor student, a lift a few times. Country folks looked out for each other back then and no doubt many still do.

Michael had been accepted into his chosen course, but at the eleventh hour he told you that he wouldn't be going to Melbourne. I can still remember his words, 'My parents have bought a large block of land just outside Ararat, and we are going to start a vineyard.'

That news was a big shock to you, and you were very disappointed. But you kept a stiff upper lip and dutifully went off to Melbourne alone. The only saving grace in the whole situation was that you had your older cousins living not far from the hostel, so it felt a bit less intimidating.

Coming from small towns in Victoria to a big noisy, fast-paced city was a big change for all the country kids. You had a slight advantage over some of them though, as you had visited Melbourne many times when you were a little girl when your family lived in Ballan. Your Granny had taken you on adventures to visit friends and your parents had taken you children to the Melbourne Zoo, to the Puffing Billy Railway and to stay with friends who lived in Springvale.

It was daunting finding your way from Armadale by bus into the city, then either catching a tram up Swanston St to the University or, as you mostly did, walk the several city blocks because you were too shy to ask anyone which number tram you should catch. Having walked everywhere you went, as your family had no car, it was normal for you to walk and it kept you fit.

One of the biggest challenges you had in those first weeks was that on Orientation Day you had met a girl called Jenny, who like you, was going to be doing the same course and living in the same hostel. She was a total geek, and you didn't particularly like her. So when you arrived at the hostel on the first day, your heart sank when you discovered that she had arrived early and had organised to be your roommate.

Zanny, the polite and caring soul that you were, you didn't say a word because you felt sorry for her. She came from a small dusty town up in the Wimmera and most likely hadn't been to the city as much as you had. Your kind heart meant that you were to endure several months of hell as the geek would wash her waist-length red hair at 10 pm and sit up until about 2 am whilst it dried. The lamp on her desk would be burning until she deemed her hair dry enough to lie down on. You meanwhile were becoming more and more sleep-deprived and more miserable by the day.

If you had been a bit more confident, you could have asked for help from one of the hostel carers about how to talk over your exhausting issues. You might have been able to sort things out with Jenny or perhaps have moved to a different room with someone more on your wavelength. Sadly, you had little or no skills in conflict resolution, having come from a volatile family dynamic where people yelled loudly at each other rather than sitting down and talking things over.

The large lecture halls at the college were overwhelming for a young girl who had done her final year as one of 12 students doing Matriculation. Some of your classes only had two of you in them, so to walk into a hall of a few hundred people must have been very unnerving. Even a tutorial had as many people in the room as two or three classes in your old school. To go from being a big fish in a little pond was very unsettling for you and your nervousness and homesickness were making you feel like you were hungry all the time. You were spending every spare cent you had on sticky finger buns in the Uni cafe and slurping down milkshakes every day.

What a pity your Mother didn't realise that the weight you had suddenly gained in a few short months was a direct reaction to your situation. She was probably nervous that you might have been pregnant, a not uncommon occurrence even amongst Catholic schoolgirls. Didn't a few of the girls in the year below you at school get pregnant when they had been practising for their debut in the stately Town Hall? The only things they debuted in 1969 were their untimely babies.

One weekend when you went home, you broached the subject very tentatively with your parents that you were very unhappy and hating the Teacher Librarian course you were doing as your major. By then, the only subject you were enjoying and keeping up with was Speech and Drama. Those classes were held down in a beautiful old bluestone building in Bouverie Street Carlton, just a stones-throw from the old Carlton and United Brewery building. The lecturers were fun people who were encouraging and you increased your love of performance.

You had had a taste of acting at the convent schools over the years and had shone in some of the roles you had been asked to play. What a pity that your parents had the attitude that too much praise would make you, an already precocious child, big-headed. Perhaps they had been a bit overawed when you had demanded at the age of six that your teacher allow you to sing a solo at the end of year Christmas concert. It had been a very reluctant teacher who had finally allowed you to sing *Mary Had a Little Lamb*. You had a pretty voice, but you didn't have perfect pitch by any stretch of the imagination.

You did love the applause though, and that continued throughout primary school, and when you attended Loreto Convent in Portland, you thrived on the roles you had in the school plays. It meant you got to hang out at rehearsals with the senior girls. They were glamorous, and you so wanted them to notice you. In fact, you had a big crush on one girl in Form 6, called Penny. She was a boarder from Melbourne, and you wanted to grow up and have long legs and long straight hair like hers.

Your parents were quite disappointed that you wanted to leave college. They sent you outside for a while to calm down as you were a bit emotional. After a short while they called you back in and your Dad said, 'Before you do anything, your mother and I think you should speak to someone at Teachers College to find out what your options are.'

You worked out who you needed to speak to and made an appointment. The gentleman explained that you could defer from the course and reapply later that year and begin again or change your major for the following year. Of course, the studentship would cease to be paid every fortnight until you reregistered in the following February. The hostel would also no longer be available as a cheap place to live once you left college.

There were a lot of major decisions for a young woman of not quite 18 to make, and as you might know decisions are best made in a calm, clear-headed manner. You, my dear, were definitely not in either of those states. Your parents didn't want you to come back to the country either, as they were concerned that you would end up in a dead-end job in a shop or even as a factory worker in the large garment manufacturing plant on the edge of the town. They had sacrificed a lot to provide you with the best education they could afford, and they had hoped that you would make good use of it.

They had both been forced by economics at the time, to leave school at around 14 or 15 as so many of their peers had too. They had become farmhands and factory workers, and they must have been disappointed that their firstborn, a bright and sassy girl, wasn't going to become the teacher they had pinned their hopes on.

You had a lovely older friend in Melbourne, Margaret, who was a Loreto old girl from Western Australia and you and your friend Karen had been billeted with her and her husband when your class made an excursion to Melbourne from Portland a few years before.

You already had a talent for keeping in touch with people and Margaret proved to be a valuable ally to have, as she knew many influential people in Melbourne. One of her friends owned an employment agency in Collins Street, and you were soon visiting the office to take a series of tests to assess your capabilities.

You were quite attractive, and you dressed very smartly, thanks to your mother's tailoring skills. She had sent you off to college all decked out in neat home-made dresses; minis with sweet little white collars and cuffs. Some outfits made you look like a younger version of Jackie Kennedy, whose style your mother admired. That had been a source of quite a lot of your discomfort in those early days at college.

You stood out like the country bumpkin you were, as all the cool girls in the lecture rooms wore jeans, leather biker jackets, boots and sneakers and here you were, all done up in frocks and patent leather shoes. The way they wore their sleek locks was another worrisome thing as your thick wavy hair was a constant source of annoyance to you.

Do you remember the day you bought the big purple woolly hat and matching scarf in Sportsgirl? It was about the first stylish thing you ever scraped the money together to buy, and you thought it made you look like all those cool girls.

The employment agency found a clerical job for you to apply for. They couldn't put you forward for a secretarial role as the nuns in all their wisdom had deemed you and any other bright students, too smart to need typing and shorthand skills. They had ensured that you studied maths and science subjects instead, as well of course as French and Literature and Geography and History. Unless you were to study nursing or teaching, most of the knowledge you gained in the six years of secondary school will hardly be of much use, will it?

The position was at an English owned Merchant Banking company in the nominee department. They were a small team down on the third floor of one of the beautiful old Art Deco buildings which lined Collins Street back in the '70s. Formal and stuffy would be the best way to describe this firm. You must have been something of a curiosity to the English gentlemen and their polished secretaries as you flitted about the building getting share transactions approved and signed.

Someone discovered that you had been studying librarianship subjects and for several weeks you were sent down into the basement to reorganise the vast archive. You, of course never grumbled aloud about it and did it to the best of your limited abilities.

The biggest attraction about working for such a prosperous banking organisation was the wage you were offered at commencement. Zanny the 1970s were a time of big worldwide change and wages were not exempt from all that was happening in the world. They were paying you $30 per week, a whole $6 more than you had been given as a student. That was such a lot of money in 1970 to an eighteen-year-old. You felt so rich every week when the paymaster handed you the little beige envelope of cash.

You were able to find a flat with your friend Joan, and two other girls who had been looking at flats at the same time. The rent for a furnished two-bedroom flat in a relatively new block was $28 and a fourth share of that and $5 in the kitty for food, still left you with plenty of money to have a life. You could see a movie every week and buy clothes on lay-by from the trendy shops in Bourke Street and the beautiful arcades.

Your style was typical of the trends at the time, and you were best described as a Dolly Bird. That was a trend that started in London and was readily adopted by the Aussie girls – big colourful eye make-up and hair cut short at the front with tendrils hanging down at the nape. You rocked it girl, as you strode around town in impossibly high platform soled shoes, tiny waisted pants and short-cropped jackets.

The months flew by, and the decision that would change your life had to be made. The decision was, whether to go back to Teachers College or not. You probably gave it only a cursory thought though as you were headstrong and thought you knew it all.

How could you go back to living on $24 a week? How could you give up that extra $6 per week? You would have had to make sacrifices. How could you go without the outings, the clothes you were enjoying buying and wearing, the regular treats that back then $6 could buy?

You no longer wanted to live in a girl only hostel after the freedom of coming and going whenever you liked. Your parents were still living in the country, as was Michael and that relationship was at that stage still ongoing despite your dalliances with a few college boys you had met in the short time you were there.

How could you have been expected to know that the decision that was predicated on $6 a week would have such a huge impact on your whole life? If only you had thought more of the future consequences and not just the immediate gratification.

By not finishing that course and graduating with a Diploma of Education you would never have that all-important piece of paper that might have been a springboard into a career in many different areas. As you matured, you might have embraced options that at 17 you didn't even know would exist. Perhaps if you had been more confident, you might have asked for advice from adults with life experience.

The decision to keep working instead of returning to Teachers College was seemingly an easy one at the end of 1970. You were attractive, well-groomed, well-spoken and articulate, and you were always able to get work. In the buoyant economy of the '70s you had choices as to where you would work, and if you tired of the work as you so often did, there was always another firm which would hire you.

You will have pangs of regret that the opportunities that a Diploma of Teaching with a Speech and Drama major would have offered, were not an option for you. You will think about going back to study, but by the time you have got the travel bug out of your system and returned to Australia as a young married woman, a family will come along. Three children in two years and even working outside the home won't be an economically viable option until they are all at school. Then the mortgage will dictate that you must work to keep things afloat, 'Life happens while you are making other plans' to paraphrase a popular, John Lennon quote.

Zanny dearest there is no way you could have known that the decision you made then with the knowledge available to you at the time, would make such an indelible mark on your life. You have soared through life, revelling in many and varied occupations. Your thirst for knowledge has led you to undertake many courses, most of which have enhanced your everyday life. Whilst they may not have afforded you the lifestyle of the rich and famous when you look back you will realise that you have indeed lived a full and satisfying life.

Looking back as I am now, the best advice I would have given you at 18 is, don't think you know it all. Ask for direction from people with more experience, speak up and look ahead a few years and realise that sticking at your studies might open doors that at 18 you can't imagine possible.

You are to be congratulated though that you had the pluck to go off out into the big wide world at the tender age of 17. You had the courage to keep striving for better working conditions, and you never sat back and watched life from the sidelines. It has been great reflecting upon those times so long ago and seeing how far the timid country girl you were has come. Well done you indeed.

Casting my mind back to write this letter to you has brought into focus how much I have struggled all through my life to accept advice from others. Being confident in your own self is a valuable asset. However, by writing this letter, I have recognised the lessons that my younger self can teach me now. I will take the advice I wish you had taken then and make it part of my life now. Thank you, Zanny.

In Light & Love

Suzanne aka Granny Zanny

Breaking Through

Lisa Jane Hussey

If you want change in your environment, the change starts with you.

Lisa Jane Hussey

A Message To Your Younger Self

Standing brave up against the back of the cubicle door with my head tilted down, I'm staring at the object that determines my future. My temperature is rising, heating my body. I feel a warmth growing from my stomach up to my chest, and before it hits my throat, it's on fire. My beating heart becomes more prominent, louder and faster. Instead of my breath becoming shallow and quick-paced, breathing deeply in and calmly blowing out slowly, calms me. It's the only part of me I can control.

Everything around me is at a standstill. I can no longer hear the vibrant young friends chatting about their favourite perfume or the encouraging mum teaching her daughter how to wash her hands. The silence gives me the space to think.

I'm not puzzled by what has happened. I know when. I know where. I know why. Figuring out what to do next is the baffling part. My mind and body are not communicating. I can feel the disconnection. As my body waits for the signal, I feel my eyes moving side to side, working out where to go or who to speak to. Yet, all I see is my hand holding the stick. I'm focussed. I'm focussed on those little pink lines, vertical and horizontal, making the most perfect straight plus symbol.

Why pink? Why not blue? Why not green, or purple or brown or orange! Does the colour even make a difference to the experience? I'm standing alone in a public toilet at my local shopping centre holding this stick telling me I have to make the decision of my life. OMG, I'm only 17! Who cares what colour this plus symbol is.

Instantly feeling the anger building within, it emerges guiding me to make a move. I know exactly what my next step is. I throw the stick into the sanitary bin, getting out of the cubicle as fast as I can. With a turn of the lock, I feel free, momentarily escaping the reality of what destiny holds for me. I proceed to walk through a line of women and children waiting to use the bathroom. Without eye contact or acknowledging a thank you, I step aside allowing each person to move forward. I'm determined to get out. I'm out.

Leaving that congested bathroom is the least of my worries. Scurrying through the white tiled hallway into the shopping centre, more people confront me and a new level of anxiety surfaces. I have to get out. I have to get out of this shopping centre. I know where I have to go. Focussing on the path that leads me out into the carpark, I arrive at the bus station. Searching around, looking up at each timetable and map, I figure out which bus to take.

Waiting for this bus is nothing compared to waiting for the school bus. I don't want this one to come soon. Take your time bus. I don't want to light up a cigarette to prove Murphy's Law this time. I hope it rains. I hope the weather changes. I hope I cool down.

It's a beautiful sunny day. But I'm not standing in the sun absorbing the rays for leisure. I'm in despair. Standing still. Rounded shoulders. Staring out into the distance. I wait for the bus I do not want to come. Though, it's the only way to get me far away from here.

Looking at my watch, checking the time and re-looking at the timetable, I lose my spot at the front of the line. I don't care. It's not one of those days I want to sit in the back hanging out with the cool kids. Laughing with the boys at their ridiculous hormone-driven comments fully knowing they are just trying to win us girls over. No, thank you. I've already been won over. And look where that got me; waiting at a bus stop with no idea.

One. One dollar ten. One dollar sixty.

It's a mad rush to get on the bus. No one has any common sense to be patient and let the passengers out first before we jump on. Being the last person has its advantages. There's always a free seat at the front, and that's exactly where I want to sit. Right near the driver. I need to feel secure. I need to feel safe. If anything happens to me, I know the driver can see me clearly. While I feel pain in my soul, I somehow know he will take care of me. I have never looked forward to greeting a bus driver as much as today. He will help me get to where I need to be.

Boarding the bus, I hand over the last of my coins, an exact amount for the two-hour fare. One dollar sixty. There is no way I need more time for this adventure. No, it's not an adventure. I correct myself. An adventure is meant to be exciting. It is unusual and daring, but no way is it exciting. This is a getaway, one where I'm breaking free from confinement.

Sitting with poise in the single-seat adjacent to the driver, I look into the carpark on my left and watch the stationary cars get smaller as we drive out onto the main road. I speak with the driver about the street I'm travelling to. I explain to him how far the house is from the main road once we make a turn into the street without giving too much away. My calm and collected demeanour isn't fooling him, though. He knows something is amiss. He picks up on my inexperience. I don't ride the bus alone other than going to school and home. A one way run, up and back.

I question him about the route. It's soon going to turn off into a side street and travel back to the shopping centre. My internal pressure gauge starts to rise. I'm not starting all over again. I'm not going back to that place. I need to move forward. He tells me to hop off at the next stop, as it is the last one on the route. Buses don't always stop at every stop unless the driver is notified. I don't communicate with him for fear of putting myself in more mental chaos. The look of confusion gave it away, and the driver insisted again. He slows down, stops, opens the front door and waits.

Looking at me with reassurance, this is the right decision.

OK.

I get up. I move away from the seat and tread carefully down the step onto the road. No words leave our mouths; just a fair exchange of energetic empathy. I am grateful for his help. He knows I am grateful. As the door closes behind me, I take a deep breath in, and as the bus drives off, I breathe out.

Here I am, now standing in front of a Milk Bar contemplating what to do. I haven't travelled much further by the looks of it. From a shopping centre to a mini-mart. Shall I call someone? It's obvious I need to call someone. But who do I contact? Mum? My boyfriend? It feels like I'm a contestant on a television game show. I bet if this was a story, a chapter in a book, the audience would clearly see what I need to do next.

My feet feel like they are immersed in the concrete footpath. They feel heavy and stuck, just like my choice of working out who to call. Maybe I don't need to call anyone. I could just head further down the street to my boyfriend's house. But what if he's not home? That would just add to the confusion in knowing where to go next. But what if he is home? Would I even know how to break the news to him?

I shake my head, look up to the sky and realise I didn't even stop to think at the shopping centre before jumping on the bus. I just wanted to get out of that hell hole as quickly as possible. That was my mission. And now, I give myself a pausing moment to decide. Music plays softly in the background of my mind.

I decide to phone a friend. I'm calling him.

The thing is, I have a mobile phone. It's sitting on my bedside table charging. When I left to go to the shops, I didn't foresee the result to be positive. I went into flight mode. I didn't think. Period. Oh, how I wish I had *that* right now!

He has a mobile phone too. Do you think I even remember his number off by heart? I should. I'm 17 and majoring in specialist maths. What good am I if I can't remember 10 numbers!

I need to create a plan. I'm calling his home. Let's see if he's there first. Baby steps. I lift my right foot and take a step forward. Heading toward the Milk Bar, I will walk in and ask to use their phone. Leading to the front door, it looks quite big compared to my petite stature and heavy enough to push me back if I go at it with full force. Do I even have the energy to push it open? I surprise myself with one swing. The door feels light as a feather. I take a further four steps and make room for the door to swing behind me. It closes slowly. It sounds heavy. I have more energy than I thought.

Across the room, I hear a muffled sound. The shop assistant stands up from packing a shelf behind the counter. I ask them if they have a phone I can use. They point to the public phone. I have no money. I wish I had more. I wish money didn't control me. I'm frightened. I don't know what to do. The shop assistant can see how anxious I am. They can see I'm in trouble. They open the till and pull out two coins. They hand it over to me. 40 cents. I walk over to the blue public phone. It's standing low. It's distinctive. I look at it for a while. The shop assistant is behind me, not close, but close enough to feel her eyes watching my back.

I lift the black handle and put it to my ear. I hear nothing, so I put the coin into the slot, and a sound of a dial tone appears. I press the little silver squares with numbers imprinted on them. They are hard to press, jamming on the sides. I wait. It starts to ring. My stomach hurts. Oh no, his mum will answer the phone! I'm cool. I'm calm. I can do this. I'm an actress. I study drama. I know how to role-play. I have been on stage. I have performed. My family even think I am a great actor. I can do this.

His mum answers the phone, and I die. I'm trying my best to be cool. I ask if he's home. He isn't. I go quiet thinking what to say or do next. She asks if I'm ok and I say, 'Yes, I am ok.' There are no other words to speak. I say goodbye. She says goodbye. I hang up. I stand at the blue payphone, rounded shoulders, head tilted down and feeling pain in my soul. I thank the shop assistant and walk out of the Milk Bar.

Staring out onto the main road, I'm frozen. I think twice about what to do. What choice do I have now? My solar plexus is on fire, my anxiety increases and my blood is boiling. Adrenaline kicks in; fight or flight.

RUN.

I run. The trees are tall. The nature strips are short. I have no idea what else to think of other than to run. A surge of bliss rushes over me, and a sense of freedom fuels me.

I'm running as fast as I can, like the speed of light. Everything around me is moving so slowly. I can feel the wind against my body. It's not a windy day. I am making the wind. Every worry flies away. My arms, like a secret weapon, are powering every movement. I am alert.

Crossroad. Right. Left. Straight road.

I pick up speed. I feel like Cathy Freeman. 400 meters. I sprint. Straight run. Why can't I ever run like this for school athletics? Nothing is stopping me now. No car is pulling out of the drive-ways. No children are riding their bikes. I just need to get home. The faster I run, the sooner I will get there. I'll figure it all out then.

The trees look shorter and more dense with leaves. The nature strips are wider. I'm running for my life. For two lives. I'm not puffed out. I have so much energy. I see the main road in the distance in front of me, the block where I live. I run past the primary school. I run past the high school. I run through an abandoned block of land and make it to my street. I run to the front door of my house.

I'm not short of breath. I'm not exhausted. I take my key and insert it in the hole perfectly. I'm not clumsy today. I'm precise. On point. Sharp. I lock the front door behind me and march straight to the bathroom. I need to be sure this is true. I close the bathroom door behind me. I sit on the toilet, with my pants hanging at my ankles, I pull out of my pocket another stick. A second one. The second one. I pee. And then I wait. I dress myself in anticipation. I'm not watching it this time. I'll wait the full three minutes, and then I'll look at it.

Standing brave up against the back of the bathroom door with my head tilted down, staring at the object that will determine my future. Positive again.

I slide down the door, like a scene out of a movie, bending my knees as I sit on the cold tiles. I feel it's coolness soothing my body.

Thoughts finally run through without having to search for them. Opportunities. Challenges. Resolutions. I don't want to be a single mum living in Epping! I want to raise my child. I don't want my mum raising my child while I go to school. Work! I don't want to work just yet. I already have a part-time job. I want to study! I want an education! I want all the answers, even the answer for when I don't have an answer.

A vision from my past flashed before my eyes. I will never forget that day. My mind sees a teenage girl from school pushing her baby in a pram up the hill on Cooper Street, going to the Plaza. Her pants were hipster leggings, and her butt crack was showing. As a result of her pants being so low, the bottoms had been stepped on from the back and the material worn, leaving a curved cut out. Standing still, her hem would have sat evenly over her shoes, like bell bottoms. She was walking, fast-paced up a hill and those bells were flapping about like sails on a windy day. So unattractive to me.

I judged her. I thought to myself, 'Pull your pants up! Where's the self-respect?' I felt she should have been on the bus with me going to school. I don't want to become that person.

I start to calculate my thoughts. When I ran from the Milk Bar, I felt alone. I felt I was going to do it on my own. I ran so fast, the world around me slowed down as I sped through the side streets to get home. Now I am home, and no one is here. I should feel lonelier, but I don't.

I'm only a few weeks shy of completing my VCE, and I have a bun in the oven. Shock horror! How will I get through this?

I make a vow to myself. I will prepare myself to be the best mum I can be for my future child! I will pause the moment. I will educate myself. I will find all the answers.

I repeat my vow and start to hear a faint noise at the front door of my home. I hear steps. I hear a person. I listen more carefully. Attentively. I wonder if it's my parents. It couldn't be. They drive in the garage and walk through the side door. Could it be my sister? I hear the handle turn and the door swing open.

It's time for me to get up. I have made my decision. It was a difficult decision and one which I thought I would never need to make. But I know what to do. I stand up. Take a deep breath in and breathe out as I stand up tall, shoulders back. The sound of the other person becomes clearer as they walk down the hallway. I face myself. It's time I start the next chapter of my life. This is the turning point.

I open the door and there stands me, my future self. Her hand reaching out to hold mine. I hold her hand, and as I take my first step, we both look at each other, and I feel her essence. She says; 'Come on, we've got work to do. Let's go!'

From that moment, it was like my future self had come back to help my younger self. She took my hand and together we made an amazing turn-around to my life. I went on to complete my VCE fully expecting to follow my heart and attend university studying behavioural sciences.

I had a couple of twists and turns during my education journey. Whilst working to pay for my university fees, I found a love for beauty and skin therapy. There was a significant gap between science and beauty in the industry, and that's when I began my holistic path. With my upbringing in hospitality, I provided a service for people to feel like they were a guest in my home, comfortable and open to share their vulnerabilities. That way I was able to help them achieve their desired results by treating the cause, not just the symptoms.

My late teens and early twenties were a stage of building knowledge. Once I hit my quarter-life crisis at 25, I started to question my purpose. I wanted to know more about why we behave the way we do. I wanted to also understand my own emotions. I had a sense that I wasn't a child anymore, yet standing independently was unsettling.

I attended my first personal development seminar of many, and my whole outlook on life shifted. I awoke to the ability of loving all the parts of myself unconditionally. I became more sure about who I was, and I grew a confidence I had once known so well on that day when I was 17. During one of the seminars, we shared our greatest challenges in our lives, and I was amazed to learn I wasn't alone. So many others experienced teenage pregnancy, either directly or through their partners, family or friends. I didn't feel ashamed anymore. A burden lifted from my shoulders. It gave me hope that one day I will experience motherhood, on my terms.

In my late 20's, I felt a sense of accomplishment I wanted to maintain in my life. I had a successful and well-established business. I was following a wealth principles system. Money no longer controlled me. I understood where it came from, and I knew how to get it. I wanted to step up and start working on a new achievement. This is when I knew it was time to meet a man to enjoy life with.

I used the online dating sites well before it was popular as it has become today. People were quite shocked when they came to learn of my method of meeting new people. That's when a work colleague introduced me to their friend. It was love at first sight.

A mouth-dropping moment. We dated. We got engaged. We married.

But I never imagined what was going to happen to me next. I thought my past would never repeat itself. There I stood, in a similar setting, in a bathroom. I held a pregnancy test in my hand with that glowing plus symbol. My instant reaction was tears running down my face. I was so sad. I cried silently.

I whispered to myself, 'This is the beginning of the end. I'm going to be a single mum living in Epping!'

My husband was sitting in the lounge, with his back facing me. I peeked out of the bathroom to check on him. In that moment, I called upon my 17-year-old self for strength. It was the right timing. I was educated. I had a well-established business where I could work from home. I had all the answers. I was ready. But watching his back sitting on the couch was the saddest part of my excitement. I was in an abusive relationship.

It was just a couple of weeks prior, I asked him if we should hold off having children. We could, instead, work on building a solid foundation of trust within our marriage. But who was to know I already had a bun in the oven.

After wiping my tears, I filled myself with courage and headed out to tell him the news. He was in disbelief and wanted me to do another test to be sure. His reaction was more about fear rather than excitement; the fear of the unknown. A place I had experienced.

However, I had over a decade to work on myself and prepare for motherhood. Even though the trust wasn't there between us, I had full trust in knowing I would provide for this little human and give them the best life I knew I could.

From that moment, no matter how much work we put into our marriage, it was doomed to end. It was a time of letting go, time to disperse what no longer served me. I drew the strength from my younger self during the hardest and most challenging times. She was someone I called upon when I needed support, encouragement and bravery. She faced a life-changing turning point alone and it was ideal for her, as she found her strength in solitude. She made her choice without being told what was right or wrong from others. She made a choice based on who she wanted to be.

The final year of my marriage was the hardest. I was judged. I was made to believe I was not good enough. No matter how many times I stood tall, I was knocked down. Verbally. Emotionally. Mentally. Physically. Finding the courage to leave the relationship was the easy part. The hard part was finding a clear passage to walk through in one piece without a scratch. I took action and escaped my abusive marriage. I thought all would get better from then on. I thought disconnecting from everyone who didn't have faith in me would be enough. The most difficult challenge was the healing process. My nervous system was fragile. My daughter's digestive system compromised.

In my mid 30s, soon after my separation, I was in either fight, flight or freeze mode every second of the day. I was super busy from the moment I woke up to the last minute before going to sleep. I thought I had no time to rest. Stress led me to consume processed foods which depleted my organs of energy. Then chronic fatigue kicked in to force me to slow down. It tried to take me away from my child and my business. In my darkest hour, I thought I would never live a life full of vitality. What got me through it was the vow I made when I was 17; to be the best mum I could be for my child.

This new moment was a place to start afresh. Build. I tapped into my younger self and brought out the student. I researched and found a way to heal the trauma. I took refuge in food, plant-based whole foods, and followed a system called the chi cycle lifestyle, which fuelled my organs and nourished my energy. Switching modes for when I ate breakfast, lunch and dinner created a foundation for my healing modality. Tweaking my morning, noon and night routines opened up limitless opportunities for time.

I was no longer in a dark place, depressed with no vision of my purpose. When dealing with trauma, the mind needs a healthy body to help work through it. A healthy body can lead the mind to no longer perceiving life as hectic and unbearable.

My younger self gave me that idea; to free myself of confinement and create a space for growth. When I reach out to my younger self, I have one clear message; thank you! Whenever I spend quality time with her, I show my gratitude for her strength, her bravery, her intuition and her knowingness.

Lisa Jane,

My dear younger self. When you were faced with the greatest challenge of your life, you allowed yourself to make a decision all on your own. Even with distractions, you didn't allow anything hanging over your head stop you. You took action. The majority of people in this world can't see they have this freedom. They can't see the world clearly as freedom is invisible to them. There are so many obstacles in their way, and the thing is, they actually put them there.

You, however, had the ability to use your challenges as a way to strengthen who you were and it guided you to where you were going. Because of you, I am now helping people to rise above their health and wellbeing challenges. This is called purpose.

When I lose my way, with you, I am always found. You made an imprint. And when I am in times of distress, I call upon your strength and I am able to breakthrough.

Thank you.

Continuing to grow, Older Self.

Glimpses Of Me

Kathy Zisiadis

Trust and have faith in your journey. Everything happens for a reason; it prepares you for your future path.

Kathy Zisiadis

So many endless nights with the twinkling city lights as a backdrop, we played hide and seek in the streets of Brunswick East in Melbourne. Times were different back then. They were simple. There were fewer cars on the roads and no social media or technology to consume our minds and life. Life was simple but fun! We were in someways carefree and looked forward to those long summer nights after school.

Local kids of all different ages would gather at sunset just after dinner at the end of the street, and the fun and games would begin. With the sound of 'You're it!' the excitement mounted and the chase was on. But my world as a child was not always fun and games, in fact, at times it felt fearful, daunting and overwhelming.

Being the firstborn child to immigrant parents had many drawbacks. I was expected to act as their interpreter and translator in their everyday affairs, particularly during traumatic situations. This became overbearing for me and a huge burden to carry as a young child. There were times when I resented the fact that my parents couldn't speak fluent English, and I especially disliked their accent.

My mother was born in a small village called Dafni, near Sparta in Greece. Today we have a habit of referring to it as 'Dafni land.' I recently visited Dafni land with my daughter, and I was filled with excitement thinking of the quiet and peaceful village lifestyle. No hustle and bustle, no city noise, just serenity.

I remember travelling to Dafni land as a child. I loved the countryside, clean air and little intertwining narrow paths dressed with cobblestone. Houses on each side were coloured either white, pink or orange and lined all the pathways that led to the town centre. The joyous memory of getting lost many times in this maze of paths still brings a smile to my face. It was in Dafni land that my love for nature and gardens began.

My daughter did not share the same sentiments and was not the least bit impressed on our recent visit to Dafni land. You could see the sheer frustration on her face and in her body language, as she demanded to leave. 'I'm not staying. When is the next bus out of here?' My daughter's frustration soon passed when she found out my aunt, Mum's sister, had kindly organised Internet and WIFI connection at her house in anticipation of our visit. Oh, how life has changed. My life as a child does take me back to those times spent in my mum's village. I felt free, no responsibilities, no interpreting and translating obligations, no spotlights. I could be an introverted little girl.

Back then, my grandfather paid for my mother to complete a dressmaking course at a technical school in Sparta, but job opportunities in Dafni land and the surrounding villages were very limited. In 1965, along with her older brother and sister and thousands of other immigrants, my mother boarded a large ship called 'The Patris' and ventured out to Australia. Subsequently, my father's destiny was no different.

My father was born in Chalkida in Evia but grew up in the city of Athens, Greece. Times were difficult and very different back then for my parents. Children attended school but simultaneously worked from a young age to help meet the financial needs of the family. My father was no exception. Being raised in a city, he was lucky enough to complete his education and graduate from high school. However, his involvement in the family business from a young age had unforeseen consequences for his family. He had lost interest, and instead of taking over the reins of the family business, he wanted to travel abroad and seek adventure and fresh opportunities in another country. 'Australia' was his promised land.

Both my parents had a strong work ethic and worked in factories, making an honest living. They worked hard like most European immigrants and contributed to building Australia and making it the great country it is today. My father always talked about those missed opportunities available to him in the city of Athens and somewhat regretted not continuing to further education. So he would constantly state 'My daughters will become highly educated and I will not have it any other way!' Because I loved learning, from a young age I took that on board and was determined to study at university someday.

I always dreamed of becoming a teacher. I strived for this dream and worked hard towards this goal. I succeeded in becoming a corporate trainer, and later a Secondary School teacher, fulfilling my teaching aspirations.

My parents did the best they could with the tools they had at the time. Looking back now, I understand the difficulties they confronted; including language barriers, cultural differences and religious differences. Coming to Australia meant leaving part of their heritage behind and trying to assimilate into the Australian way of life. It was a huge sacrifice for anyone to make. They needed to learn a new language and build a new life for themselves. Times were not easy for a young couple starting a new family in a new country, and there were many ripple effects on their children.

As a young child, I felt a responsibility to help my parents overcome the barriers they faced and stepped in during especially tough times. However, times were not always difficult. I recall many fun and joyous memories with the family car.

The family car was a very long white sedan, a Chrysler Valiant which was my dad's pride and joy. My much younger sisters and I had a seating arrangement in the big white car. I would strategically sit behind the passenger's seat to avoid the thin white nicotine smoke, which often unintentionally blew into your face if you were directly behind the driver. My middle sister would sit behind the driver and my younger sister was stuck sitting between us. I say stuck because on numerous occasions, the battle was on. My younger sister would attempt to swap seats with us, but again and again, she would lose the battle.

We loved the good old valiant and the wonderful trips my parents took us on, but my favourite feature of the car was the little white pom-pom trimming carefully placed along the top of the rearview window. This harmless decorative trimming I dare say became our *vehicle* for punishment.

We loved staring out the back of the car window watching the hundreds of little white pom-poms, the size of peas, as they swayed and bounced with the movement of the car. The pom-pom trimming framed the external environment just like a moving picture and in some ways made the environment more aesthetically pleasing to look at on those extra-long journeys.

The Chrysler Valiant was a crucial part of my childhood with fun times spent travelling. In all its glory and complete with little white bouncing pom-poms, she took us to magnificent Australian landscapes. We visited Bendigo, Lakes Entrance, Phillip Island, Rye, Sorrento, Geelong, Renmark, and Mount Buller, to name a few. I especially loved drives along The Great Ocean Road to Queenscliff, Torquay, Anglesea, and all the way to Lorne, Portland even Adelaide.

But all this ended one early Sunday morning in 1977 when I stood in front of our black and white T.V in shock! My eyes were transfixed on the screen. The horrific image of 'a half-burnt white vehicle' that had overturned on the open fields of Wangaratta, immediately captured my attention. A graphic image of the wreckage confirmed my fears. A half-burnt trimming of white pom-poms hanging at the rear car window looked familiar. I felt sick. I felt powerless. In that moment the telephone rang. The police confirmed that my dad had been in a car accident.

Travelling to Wangaratta, outside NSW by train with my mother and sisters was a horrible experience. Although we knew my father was alive and lying in a hospital bed with a broken collar bone, broken arm and severe bruising, it felt like we were mourning. Despite the fact that my father's injuries were non-life threatening, my mother cried in the train carriage for the whole two and a half hour trip, and I found myself not only consoling my mother but also comforting my sisters who were scared and turned to me for security.

My father, who was the President of the Greek club of Evia in Melbourne, was heading to Sydney with members of the committee for business. Being the designated driver, he veered off the road to avoid a collision with an oncoming interstate truck driver who accidentally entered into their lane. The Chrysler Valiant overturned and rolled five times. With every roll a passenger was mercilessly thrown out of the vehicle and into the fields of Wangaratta before the car burst into flames. My father and his passengers were lucky to have survived.

This traumatic event was not easy to overcome. It put a strain on the whole family. I remember my parents arguing for the first time. We spent a couple of weeks in a hotel near the hospital where my father had been admitted, as he was discharged only when he was well enough to travel back to Melbourne. What followed was many months of rehabilitation for my father and enormous responsibilities for me. Being firstborn, I was expected to take charge, deal with authority figures and help the family. At the time, being young, this felt overwhelming, scary and frustrating.

I now know being firstborn is special and it's a blessing in disguise. It's a blessing because as the eldest child, I was expected and compelled to confront various life situations, and was trusted with immense responsibility, and this helped me to build strength, character and ultimately self-esteem. I was the one with more experiences under my belt, more wisdom, courage and thus more respect; I was a role model for my siblings.

Now, I can appreciate that I had an important role to help the family, to show the way and to carve the right path for my siblings to follow. I was the rock during difficult times and the one to provide emotional support no matter how big or small their problems. Today, I still have that respect, and my siblings look up to me.

Nonetheless, during those formative years in my childhood, all I felt was that somehow it was my responsibility to fix things, and in some ways, even my fault when things went wrong. The other time I felt this most deeply was when my father was attacked.

It was a cold, dark winter's night in 1980. It was a school night, and I was sitting at my desk in my PJs, quietly studying for a Year 7 Math test I had the following day. My bedroom was quite large considering our home was a Victorian single front terrace with 12-foot ceilings. Positioned in the middle of my room against the wall was my bed facing the bedroom door. Adjacent to my bed was my desk complete with a hutch and shelves just like a teacher's desk, and on the opposite side was my dressing table. My bedroom was my sanctuary, where I listened to music, relaxed, studied and enjoyed peaceful times away from my younger and at times, annoying sisters.

The night is quite vivid. It was about 11 pm when I heard banging on the front door. I was almost done solving an algebra math equation. I knew it was my dad because he usually came home from shift work at that time. However, the banging on the door was unusual. My dad had a key to the house, so why was he banging on the front door?

Puzzled, I tried to block out the noise and complete my task. But the banging got louder. My sisters were in the second bedroom of the house, sleeping. At this time, my mother was in the kitchen at the back of the house, routinely preparing a late supper for my dad and couldn't hear the noise at the front door. But there was no ringing, no soft knocking, just loud banging.

Bang! Bang! Bang! My pencil suddenly dropped out of my left hand, and with my heart racing, I jumped out of my desk chair and quickly moved towards my bedroom door. With hesitation, I entered the corridor. The corridor lights were on and straight ahead were bloody palms pressed against the frosted glass and my dad's silhouette behind them. I felt my heart skip a beat as my body became numb and went into slow motion mode. The long corridor of our Victorian single front terrace home suddenly appeared endless and it felt like I would never reach the end. Why was it taking so long to get to the door? It was surreal, like an out of body experience.

Reluctantly, I opened the door and my father, with blood gushing out of his face, fell into the house. Towering behind him was a tall man with black beady eyes and clenched bloodied fists with brass knuckles. For a few seconds, I froze. I felt, once again, powerless. The tense expression on his face and the loud, aggressive tone in his voice said it all. This was an act of evil! Next to him stood an enormous beast barking relentlessly, just like its owner. It was a black/brown German Shepherd which I recognised. It was our next-door neighbour's dog.

By now, my mother had rushed out from behind me and desperately pushed me out of the way to safety. She grabbed my father's shoulders and bravely dragged him into the house, shutting and locking the door behind her. At the top end of the corridor lay our family's protector, my dad, in a pool of blood on the hard timber floor. Semi-consciously he mumbled, 'Call the police.' I stood in shock sobbing and shaking a few metres away from the phone. My younger sisters were now peaking from their bedroom door looking on in horror as the drama unfolded. My mother was nursing my dad's wounds, and I knew as the eldest child, I had to do my bit to help the family through this crisis. At that point, I knew once again that I had to be strong because my parents needed me now more than ever before. I needed to compose myself and call the police immediately.

Our telephone was sitting halfway down the corridor on a little table against the wall. Starring at the dark green phone, my hands were shaking. It wasn't as simple as asking 'Siri' to dial the police. Back in the day, there were no mobile phones, no internet, no Facebook, no Snapchat, no WiFi. People had to talk to each other to communicate, and that was if you were lucky enough to own a telephone. Luckily we had a phone. I had to insert my index finger into the small round numbered holes in the hard-plastic dial and move my finger in a circular motion to dial the police. I had to do this three times to dial emergency 000.

The police came an hour later. They questioned my father, who spoke broken English. They assured us that after speaking to the man, he was apologetic and would not do it again. That's it. No arrest, no consequences.

The man who attacked my dad was known to police. He slurred swear words at us which I didn't understand at the time, but have now come to realise they were very denigrating words with racial undertones. It was our neighbour, a Turkish man who was renting the house next door with his wife and daughter. There had been multiple incidents and numerous times when he would get drunk and get into domestic altercations with his wife. Police had been called to his address before. He abused alcohol and other substances but never in a million years did we anticipate he would launch an unprovoked attack on my father and our family.

Once the initial shock of that violent crime against my father had passed, and the dust had settled, my parents no longer felt safe in our neighbourhood and made a very difficult decision to sell our home and move to another suburb or overseas. My father had grown tired of constantly looking over his shoulder when coming home or going to work, and during his absence from the home, my mother had increasingly become too frightened to be alone with young kids. I, on the other hand, spent the best part of that year blaming myself. If only I had opened that door sooner.

I remember being heartbroken and my world falling apart when my parents broke the news to the three of us. Moving away from my neighbourhood, away from my school, away from my friends and away from my home, was devastating to me. It meant making a new start in a new place with new people, which was terrifying. What if I didn't fit in? What if I was the only student with ethnic parents? What if I was the only left-handed student in my new class? Would I be bullied again by the school system for being left-handed?

Although I was devastated being the eldest and feeling partly responsible for what happened to my father, I felt a sense of responsibility and pressure to help the family through this transition. At the time, my sisters didn't fully understand the magnitude of the situation, so they were more accepting of my parents' decision to move. Time and time again, I accompanied my parents to appointments with travel agents, real estate agents, bank managers and acted as their interpreter and translator. I was very torn during this part of my life; living with the guilt of what had happened to my father and dealing with the ripple effects of this incident.

The trauma was not my fault. Now I know that. But sometimes it was difficult not to resent the fact that my parents were immigrants.

I remember standing with a white plastic shopping bag in my hand next to my mum in a butcher shop. Next to my mother stood a tall, pretty lady, in dark blue jeans with a slender build, long blonde hair and piercing blue eyes. I had never seen hair like that, and I found myself admiring her luscious golden locks as they hung halfway down her back. Laughter disrupted my focus and admiration. My mother accidentally asked the butcher for a 'kitchen' instead of a 'chicken'. On either side of this pretty lady leaned two disobedient young boys, about my height, who looked at me and laughed the whole time while teasing and mimicking my mother's broken English.

Suddenly an awful word came out of one of the boy's mouth, 'Wog.' I didn't quite understand its meaning, but it made me feel ashamed and hurt. I had no idea these nasty words could have such an impact on me and cause me pain. Why was I different? Why were my parents Greek?

At the time, I remember feeling alienated, but I now understand that having Greek heritage enriched my life in ways I couldn't appreciate at the time.

Although I experienced racism as a child, I was fortunate to have learnt two languages and experienced two cultures simultaneously. Both of these experiences have helped build my character, strengthen my courage and determination and made me the person I am today.

But back then, it wasn't easy being different.

Back then, left-handed school children had to deal with physical restraint and bullying and were forced to write with their non-dominant hand. Every single teacher I had (even at Greek school) used retraining methods on me, such as tying or immobilising my left hand. My brain had associated the pencil with fear and learning initially had become difficult for me.

I remember sitting anxiously at the kitchen table. I was waiting for my dad to help me with my Greek school homework and contemplating how I would get through the lesson without being smacked on my left hand. Every single time, I had to make a conscious effort to pick up my pencil with my right hand. Again and again, I subconsciously found myself writing with my left. My brain was in charge, and I had no control. It felt natural and comfortable. Left felt right! As a child, I could not understand what I was doing wrong.

'Right! Are you *right* to start the lesson?' That would be my dad's subtle way of reminding me which hand I needed to use. To avoid humiliation and punishment at a very young age of six, I found myself sitting on my left hand so I would not be tempted to use it when writing. This restraint became a habit and conditioning occurred for many years.

Today, I know that left-handers make up approximately 10 per cent of the population and that handedness doesn't matter when it comes to a person's abilities or intelligence. Today research even suggests a link between being left-handed, *'a leftie,'* and being more creative, faster thinking and efficient in multi-tasking. I am aware there are left-handed Presidents; Barack Obama, Bill Clinton, George H W Bush, and Ronald Reagan. Other famous members of the left-handers club include Mahatma Gandhi, Nelson Mandela, Leonardo Da Vinci, Aristotle, Isaac Newton and Bill Gates. I couldn't possibly comprehend or appreciate such facts when I was a child.

School was not easy back then.

Today a block of townhouses and apartments sit on the corner of Albert and Blair Streets, Brunswick; a corner block once occupied by Brunswick Central Primary School. My school! I can still see it clearly in my mind. It was a majestic modern triple story building in rendered grey with floor to ceiling glass windows across the front. At the front of the school lay a massive concrete yard with basketball courts, netball courts and a cricket pitch. A colourful playground occupied the left side of the school's front yard comprising of monkey bars, swings, a sandpit and other playground equipment. The school was secured by a high barbed wire fence.

My primary school was beautiful, and one thing I remember loving about school was recess. Recess for me was a delightful milk bottle experience. When the bell rang, we all ran outside into the big concrete yard and lined up with our respective classes and waited in anticipation for our milk. The milk trucks always delivered the crates of milk bottles to the school in the early morning, so the milk bottles were there for us in time for recess.

The teachers stood at the front of the lines and one by one, students took their fresh milk bottle in an orderly fashion and moved to the back of the line. I loved those mornings. The milk was cold, fresh and delicious. Fortunately for me, one of the girls in my class would slip her milk bottle into my hand as she walked passed me to the back of the line. 'Drink up. It's good for your teeth and bones,' echoed the teacher's wise words.

Another thing I distinctively remember about primary school was the headmaster, now known as the principal. The headmaster was someone we all feared. Every single student at Brunswick Central was scared of him and rarely passed outside his office. He was a tall man, with a thin build, a moustache and glasses. The headmaster mostly dressed in a brown suit and walked around with a cane in his hand.

In the 1970's it was common for the headmaster to display his weapons in public to instil fear in the students and maintain order. The cane was a thick stick used to smack students across the knuckles for the silliest of reasons like not remembering the correct spelling of 'chrysanthemum'. Today as a teacher myself, I face such stringent rules that even a slightly raised voice at a student would land me in hot water and on the unemployment list. Today if I used the cane on a student, I would face assault charges.

One specific lunchtime at my primary school stands out to me like no other. I can recall it just like it was yesterday. It started as a regular lunchtime. I was playing tiggy with my friends when I inadvertently ran into a group of rowdy students who were fighting and who had at that second also pushed me to the ground. A deep voice bellowed, 'Right! You four, stop right now and follow me.'

I looked up to see Ms Deborah peering down at me with her short dark red hair and wrinkly skin. Her finger pointed straight at me, and I looked at her puzzled. 'But Ms Deborah it wasn't my fault,' I pleaded, but she didn't want to hear any excuses. Her face filled with rage as she pointed her finger at each one of us and ordered, 'One, two, three, four, follow me right now to the headmaster's office.' As soon as I heard 'headmaster', I froze. By the time we reached his office, I was shaking uncontrollably and had even broken into a sweat.

Outside the headmaster's office, I anxiously stood amongst the other three students waiting to learn of our fate. Tears were streaming down my face. Fear had consumed my mind and body, and I couldn't even think straight. Behind the office door, we heard Ms Deborah in her deep voice talking to the headmaster, but none of us dared to speak or even look at each other. Suddenly the office door flung open. We all looked up and standing there in his brown suit, and cane in hand was the headmaster. Ms Deborah proudly stood by his side with a smug look on her face.

At that point, a miracle was needed, and it's exactly what happened for me. One of the older students bravely stepped forward and heroically pointing at me, said, 'Please Sir, she had nothing to do with this.' 'Is that correct?' growled the headmaster. The headmaster glanced down at each one of us like we were criminals and was somewhat unconvinced. The other students nodded their heads. 'You are excused,' he said looking at me somewhat begrudgingly.

A sense of relief came over me, and I remember leaving very quickly and feeling like I had just escaped a death sentence. Freedom was just a few metres away. Until this day, I don't exactly know what happened to those students, but other students' accounts say if you entered the headmaster's office of horrors, there was harsh punishment.

Discipline was a serious matter back in the day. Spanking your kids was a common way to stop them from misbehaving. Other than the 'left hand' tap, which felt more of humiliation than a smack, I don't remember my parents spanking us, but I do remember the wooden spoon. On a few occasions, my mother threatened to smack us with the wooden spoon. If you're from a Greek background, you would know that the wooden spoon magically transformed from a cooking utensil into a weapon of punishment, in a flash. I can still remember the sound of the cutlery drawer opening, which was enough to fill me with terror. These days even the slightest slap is associated with child abuse and receives judgmental stares and looks of disgust from onlookers anywhere.

As a qualified teacher and parent, I always ensure to discipline my children in a calm matter.

Becoming a parent the first time was quite daunting. I didn't know, like so many others, what to expect. As a parent, I now know it is an ongoing learning curve and a lifelong commitment to raise a child. As a single parent of three beautiful children, it has not always been easy. I had to work hard as a corporate trainer and teacher to give my children the necessary tools for good health and well-being in life, and it has undoubtedly paid off.

Today my son and daughter, my two young adult children are thriving as law students, working part-time and pursuing their dreams. My youngest son in middle school is striving for academic excellence. I am extremely proud of my three beautiful and extraordinary children.

Parenting has been the most difficult yet rewarding job I ever had to do. Looking back, I am grateful for my childhood journey and experiences as I now understand and appreciate my parents parenting skills. I'm grateful my parents continuously gave me the opportunities as a child to find my voice and courage to build character strength and become a responsible person. It was the challenges and unfortunate serious circumstances in my childhood that gave me the tools to deal with difficult situations in my adult life. As a parent, I understand my parents' expectations and fears with me, their first child, because they were experiencing things for the first time. First fever, first steps, first day of school and the list goes on.

Life is never Polly-Anna easy. To be constantly thrust into the spotlight and forced to speak to authority figures; to translate and interpret during traumatic events; to be disciplined and singled out for no apparent reason other than being left-handed; was all very overwhelming to me as a child. I was an introvert.

Looking back I can now appreciate that these early experiences of having to find the courage to speak up helped me become who I am today. These childhood experiences transformed me from an introvert to an extrovert. Today, no matter what life throws at me, I am brave enough to confront, deal with, and act in spite of fear. And I wouldn't have it any other way.

If I knew then what I know now, I would tell myself that trauma is not your fault. It's not your fault that your father was physically attacked; nor is it your fault that he nearly died in a car accident. Don't be hard on yourself; be gentle and give yourself permission to grieve and heal.

Being unique and different is awesome; so embrace the strength in your left hand. It's fabulous you're proficient in a second language, and appreciate a second culture; you're enriched.

Don't be scared, because everything will be okay and work out exactly how it's meant to be. Try your best because your best is good enough, and remember there is no such a thing as the perfect human being.

The Young Girl Who Was Too Scared to Cry

Anne-Marie Donis

Once I discovered I was in charge of my own destiny, my dreams of freedom finally came true!

Anne-Marie Donis

I was feeling guilty once again! That was not unusual in my daily life.

This time it was about helping someone out, yet again. My mind was ticking over 'Am I really free to help or am I being obliged to help out?' That was such a dilemma for me growing up and still is. Every time I am faced with helping friends or family, I find myself looking for excuses to get out of helping or just biting the bullet and doing what people expect of me.

I can still hear my mother's words, 'You can't think about yourself. You need to put everyone else first, and help others out, no matter what,' and I always did!

However saying 'Yes' all the time was a very destructive pattern for my wellbeing and caused me a lot of stress, anxiety and most of all, guilt. This pattern became an ongoing cycle in my life. So where and when did this pattern start? Looking back at my childhood, I realised it had started from a very young age – when I was in the hospital having heart surgery at the age of nine, and all I felt was guilt.

I still remember a visit to our local GP with my dad and oldest brother. After what seemed a very long time, the GP gave my brother the all-clear for his ailments, but my dad still looked very worried and concerned about me. Surely a few spots, blisters and what looked like a case of ringworm wasn't serious. I'd had all these ailments before.

The GP wrote down a great deal of information for my dad and explained that I would have to go to the hospital the following week. I asked myself, 'Do children nine years of age go to the hospital for this?' I was very confused and unsure of what was happening.

I don't remember my parents ever talking to me about going to the hospital, but I'm sure they did. All I remember was it had something to do with my heart and that that this was a big deal for me and my family. Even though I was only nine years old, I had been to hospital several times before for oedema of the kidneys, a tonsillectomy and an operation to fix my toes, but this seemed different. This was to be one of many times in my life that I would go to a hospital for a serious illness or operation.

I was a little girl just wanting to cry out for help, but instead, I kept quiet as my mum taught me to do. All I could feel was fear of the unknown, anxiety and a sense of guilt for being sick again. When my parents and their family gathered around my parent's kitchen table talking about me and asking, 'Why is she sick again? What's wrong with her this time?' I just wanted to disappear. I felt so upset and embarrassed that something was always wrong with me. I felt guilty of being sick.

I did share the health limelight with my dear brother, who sadly passed away at the age of 38. He too was always sick, and the doctors back then couldn't give my parents a proper diagnosis, let alone any support for his illness. He was later to be diagnosed with severe epilepsy. I didn't want my parents to have two out of their five children sick or in and out of hospitals. It wasn't fair for them. They already had a serious issue dealing with my youngest brother. So why should they worry about me? I didn't feel important enough. After all, my mother said that I should focus on what other people wanted not what I wanted or needed.

If only I could tell this little girl, going through so much, that there is no reason to feel guilty. It is not your fault you are sick. You deserve just as much attention as anyone else. You are important too.

I certainly didn't feel that I was okay or important back then.

Life with my family, like any other family, had its ups and downs. As Dutch immigrants, my parents adjusted quite well in Australia.

We moved home several times and changed schools which I found very difficult while growing up. Although born in Australia, I completed kindergarten in Holland, which meant when I commenced state school in Australia, I wasn't able to speak any English. This had a big impact on my education and self-esteem.

The Young Girl Who Was Too Scared To Cry

As a young girl, my spirit would fly just like the birds and the butterflies I saw in my garden. I loved being outside, but my physical body couldn't keep up with the effervescent energy of my spirit. Forever dreaming of riding horses, climbing mountains and escaping into Mother Nature, I was always stunted by my physical incapabilities.

My dad was a man who loved nature and always loved to escape to the country, especially when he was free from work and home duties. I loved playing outside with my dad, who taught me more than I realised back then. His passion for growing plants, trees and seeing nature in its most natural state stayed with me throughout my life. My dad had unknowingly taught me how to be free and live in the moment. Yet, I also realise now that nature was also my escape from the realities of life, a few moments when I could forget about my responsibilities, my illness and feelings of guilt for being me.

My mum, on the other hand, was grounded and loved to keep the house and us kids clean. 'Spick and span,' as my mum would say after checking the daily jobs she had assigned to me. Being the oldest girl meant I was required to do all the domestic duties around the house. I didn't mind doing the jobs my mum had set for me, but I was always dreaming of being outside where my heart would sing a song of joy, and I could feel at peace.

Amongst the daily routines at home and school, I always felt very different from my brothers and sister. I didn't feel like I belonged in this family. Why? I never questioned those feelings of not belonging or connecting with others like everyone else seemed to. However, I did ask my mother if I had been adopted.

My mum had volunteered at the church and local orphanage in the town I was born in, so I thought this might be a possibility, given how different I felt from others in my family. But mum assured me that I wasn't adopted, 'I would never have brought home such an *ugly* baby!' I have never forgotten those words, and have carried them with me to this day. But no longer.

It is now time for me to let go of the hurt those words have brought me. It is time to forgive my mother and myself for allowing my mother's careless and inconsiderate remark to keep hurting me all of these years. I say to that little girl, you are beautiful, and you are loved.

However, my solution at the time was to escape. My life seemed to have everything I needed, good parents who cared, a roof over my head, food on the table each day and an education. But I felt that something was missing in my life. I wrote many poems of being free in the journal that I kept hidden under my bed. I always imagined my life to be wonderful and amazing, full of interesting adventures. However, my mum said that I was a dreamer and that it wouldn't get me anywhere in life. She told me to be organised and structured so that I would make a good wife one day. I listened to her. So, dreaming about freedom was knocked out of my head at a very young age.

It wasn't all bad. There were some happy times when, as a family, we took off in the old station wagon and had many country adventures.

I still remember the different churches we went to as a family every Sunday. One Church, in particular, stood out for me because of the beautiful gardens surrounding the church building. After Sunday mass, all the kids were allowed to play there.

The gardens were like an oasis! The small curved bridges, with water flowing underneath, flowers of all shapes and sizes with such amazing colour, all different types of trees, a path made of cobblestones which made my imagination run away with me. I was oblivious to the rest of the world. The freedom I felt was incredible, and I would pretend I was someone else living in a fantasy world with no rules. Reality didn't exist for me at that moment in time.

A few days before my heart surgery, I had many thoughts running through my mind. There was such a fear of the unknown for me. I knew by my parents' concerned faces that this surgery was a bit more serious than my previous surgeries. I needed a strategy to get through this without it affecting my parents.

I decided I could be practical like my mum which meant I had to be strong and never complain about the things life threw at you. 'Pray to God and all will be right in the world,' my mum would say.

So, I never complained and instead prayed for my life. My dad had suggested I ask our local Parish priest to bless me before I have the operation. I decided to take his advice during our practice run in the Catholic confessional box at school. It was my turn to go in and confess all my sins, but the irony was that I always made up my sins so I wouldn't get into trouble from the priest for not having any sins to confess.

I knelt down in the confessional box, which was such an eerie place, confessed my made-up sins and waited for my penance. Before I left, I quietly asked the priest if he could bless me before my heart operation. Well, that went down like a lead balloon. He yelled, 'Get out of my confessional box. How dare you ask me for a blessing. You are a sinner and a blasphemous child!' I ran out crying and so ashamed of what I had asked, only to cop a slap across the back of my head from the nun who heard all the commotion.

I shamefully sat sobbing in one of the church pews trying to get my head around the fact I wasn't even worthy of God's blessings.

I couldn't tell my parents what the Parish priest had said to me because then I would be in more trouble. So, if God wouldn't bless me, how would I survive the operation? I was scared. I felt guilty. I had convinced myself that I wasn't worthy enough to be loved by God and that if I showed any fear or worry to my mum about the operation, I would be in trouble.

If only I could tell that little girl that she is worthy of love and blessings, and not dependent or subject to the views of others, no matter who they are.

But I did not understand this back then. My daily mantra, which became embedded into my mind like a woven tapestry, sounding like a broken record: *stay strong and never talk about my true feelings.*

This is how I learnt to survive. I hid my true feelings and pretended to be strong. I never cried publicly. I didn't tell my parents what had happened in the confessional box. That way, my mum would believe I would survive this operation and Dad would feel good because he believed that the Parish priest had blessed me. My mantra seemed to serve me well and helped me survive the many critical health issues and operations I endured in my lifetime, but at what cost?

Even now, people who meet me believe I am strong and can cope with anything. They have no idea of the vulnerable person underneath, the little girl who is still inside me, repeating the mantra. But it's now time for a new mantra.

The only good thing about having to go to the hospital was getting time off school. I hated school, but I had to go. Mum would constantly say, 'The only way you are getting out of school is if you are dead, dying or in hospital.' So, going to the hospital gave me a hall pass – what a relief!

I feared failing in class, more than having a severe operation. All those rules and regulations and classwork I couldn't do. I disliked my teachers and the punishments they dished out if we made a mistake – the strap being one of them. Being at school for me was so daunting and anxiety-ridden that I would have nightmares thinking about it.

I wasn't able to follow simple instructions or pass any tests I sat, and yet my brothers breezed through school with flying colours. I was so quiet at school, and I pretended to be invisible so that the teachers would not choose me to answer a question. I was very shy and awkward and found making friends difficult. I didn't fit in at school or home, so where did I belong?

Being in the hospital was different. I got a lot of attention, and people took care of me. The operations didn't bother me, and I tolerated the pain quite well. However, the only problem was that my mum was insistent on me getting better in a hurry so I could help her at home. I didn't want to go home and then back to school because that meant the whole cycle of fear, anxiety, and guilt would commence once again.

I survived my six-hour heart operation and soon after, I was back at school, suffering abuse from the nuns who were teaching me at the time. I had fallen so far behind with my school work even though my dad had asked that I be exempt from any school work while I wasn't at school and recovering after my operation.

The nun who taught me used a cane to keep the students in line – a common practice back then. I didn't mind being hit but I was more scared of being in trouble for something I thought was insignificant. Seeing my classwork handed back to me with that awful red pen mark showing a big fat 'X' on my results still haunts me to this day.

Most of my teachers said that I would never amount to anything because I was so dumb. In my mind, this became a fact. I knew I was dumb, my mum had told me so in her own way. Her words were clear and simple; 'Your brain is like mine, dumb, and your brothers have your dad's brain, they are smart.' Why would my mum lie about that? She hadn't lied to me before, so this must be true.

Once again, I never questioned this. Why? I just never questioned anyone who was in a position of authority. My dad always worried about me growing up and believing everything I heard and was told. He told me on so many occasions 'Don't believe everything you hear, question everything in life.' I didn't follow his advice because I thought my mum had all the answers.

After making it to my tenth birthday thanks to my heart operation being successful, I was much more mobile. I could run, jump, climb so much faster and not end up out of breath or have severe blood noses.

I was also able to go with my family on our Sunday outings and many mini camping holidays to the Grampians, one of my favourite places, without falling behind.

However, I realised very quickly I no longer got blisters or rare spots on my body from touching plants or animals, so I had no real illness to stop me from going to school or an excuse to not help mum around the house. I then started feeling trapped. How do I escape school or my household duties with my mum?

I desperately wanted to go outside to escape the reality I was living.

I wouldn't have lived past 19 years of age if the local GP hadn't picked up on my severe heart condition, so why wasn't I happy now I had a second chance for longevity? I wanted to get married and have children. But I was still too young for that to be a reality. So, I kept on dreaming and writing in my journals the poetry of love and freedom. Everyone around me seemed oblivious of how boring and mundane life was. At times I just wanted to shout out to the world, 'Is this as good as it gets!' but I never did. I kept all of my thoughts, fears and sadness locked inside of me.

So why was I so happy being outside in nature and with the animals we had? Animals have such amazing unconditional love to give, and I always felt so warm and happy when I was with them. Looking back, it now makes sense.

I felt I had some freedom outside, and Dad didn't mind what we did. There were no real rules outside even in Dad's shed where all his tools were. There was no guilt with my dad. Dad's only rule was to be good at school and get an education which he believed would help us kids go forward in life.

My mum, on the other hand, was so precise and suffered from obsessive-compulsive disorder. She was a very depressed mother while I was growing up, and I had to help Dad take care of her many times. I think my mum wasn't coping with the overseas move to Australia as well as having two sick children to care for. It had taken a toll on Mum's mental and physical health. Dad was very nurturing and always made sure Mum was comfortable in life.

I never remember them arguing around us. Dad's response to any disagreement was to escape outside. The fact that Mum and Dad didn't argue or resolve issues around us kids made us all a bit vulnerable growing up.

For me, in particular, I didn't know how to problem-solve around issues that came up later in my life. I didn't know how to stand up for myself when I was being bullied at school or make a good argument for something I strongly believed in. All I knew was to escape or pretend to be strong, even though I was so scared of most things that challenged me in life.

So how could I as a child learn to find a way to have a normal conversation with other peers, siblings, who I never really connected with, to get my point across without getting angry, embarrassed or running away? How would I find my voice? This quandary stayed with me most of my adult life. It's only recently that I have started to stand up for myself without getting aggressive or running away.

The overwhelming guilt I felt was something that dominated most of my life; guilt when I was sick, especially when there were so many others in the world worse off than me, guilt at just being me, a guilt that still haunts me today.

A Message To Your Younger Self

So to that little girl who hid away and felt scared and guilty, please don't be afraid. You wore your invisible coat of armour to protect yourself so that no one would know how scared, anxious, vulnerable and guilt-ridden you were. You are safe and loved always. It's time to break free!

It's now time for a new mantra. It's time to drop the guilt and acknowledge that I am worthy of love, understanding, and respect. I accept who I am, and I don't need to escape or pretend anymore.

My new mantra is: *It's ok to show my feelings. I am good enough, and I do what makes me feel good.*

I now know I don't have to feel guilty if I get sick or say no to people if I can't do what they want me to do. I am beautiful and deserve to be loved. I know I can survive adversities that come my way. Each day brings me closer to loving and accepting who I am.

Thank you to my younger self for showing me what I need in my life now.

You were an amazing little girl who had to fight so many critical health issues, bullying, and a tough upbringing. I now realise that the love, support, and validation you were looking for only comes when you realise that you do matter and that you are good enough just the way you are.

I now realise that being my true authentic self is the only way for me to feel free and live a happy and fulfilling life. I no longer have to hide behind the armour that protected me for all those years. I now know how to get back up and move forward.

I am strong enough to cope with what life gives me. I am enough.

I am looking forward to the new me!

Our Messages

In this final chapter, the co-authors share the three main messages they have for their younger selves. This acts not only as a summary of what they have written about in their chapters, but as practical advice you can use to assist you in your own personal journey.

The authors in this book have not started their journey as experts. They are all regular people, overcoming their own difficulties and hurdles, to pursue dreams and goals, and for most of them, perhaps all, this is an ongoing process. Part of that process has been writing to their younger selves in this book.

We hope that in sharing these stories, you will be inspired to pursue your dreams and goals and reconnect with your younger self, whether that is to heal past hurts, gain strength or to remind yourself that you are loved.

What would you say to your younger self?

Antoinette Pellegrini

❖ **We all make a difference to the lives of other people, whether we realise it or not.** Sometimes we know the difference we make, whether it's helping a friend in time of need, being a positive role model to your children and others, or in my case, helping clients to achieve their writing and personal goals. Often, however, we are unaware of the impact we are making, either positive or negative. But if we proceed from a position of kindness, then perhaps it doesn't matter if we are unaware of the impact we make. My aim is to make a positive difference in whatever I do and hope to leave the world a better place because I was in it. We can all do this, and it doesn't need to be the big things. Never underestimate the impact a smile, or kind words can have. They can change a person's world.

❖ **You are good enough just as you are.** There is no need for external validation. Find the validation within yourself. Don't let others determine what good enough is. You are always enough. There is no need to compare to others; comparing yourself to others is a recipe for dissatisfaction and distress. To everyone who looks in the mirror and finds themselves lacking in some way – stop. You are good enough just the way you are. After all, you are unique, and that is your gift to the world. Love the uniqueness of who you are. Be truly yourself. That is not only enough, it is everything.

- ❖ **Seize opportunities and look forward.** Don't regret the paths not taken. You cannot change the past, but you can learn from it, change the way you think about the past and move forward. The future is waiting for you to create it. Say 'Yes' to as many opportunities as possible, and forge your own path. Be you.

Lisa Locks

- ❖ **It's okay to be different.** I came from a broken past, and that's okay. As a child, I was physically sick and troubled. I was a bird whose wings were crushed and I was getting sicker, and I didn't know why. I thought I was dumb and worthless. Through my life's journey, a key was given to me from my inner child. I opened a door and saw her sitting in the tree. She whispered to me and said, 'You are healed.' She taught me that I am different, and that is okay.

This key opened doors to truth, and it locked away fear. It gave me a vision of purpose; it unlocked a toolbox to build self-awareness and self-love. I unlocked my heart that was broken and the wounded eagle soared in the sky. Create in your mind a key to open your toolbox. Allow it to unlock any negativity and self-doubt you may sometimes have. With your own positive thinking and motivation, you can improve your self-esteem and self-worth. You're worth it.

❖ **Purpose is the key to knowing your path.** I have a purpose. This key unlocks doors and breaks through barriers. This key locks away darkness. My purpose tells me I must help children who are crushed, like my soul was, and help them be free. I sit in the tree, and she points the way, a path that leads them to me where I whisper, 'You are different, and that is okay.' You have a purpose to live and learn and share with the world. Look within the core of your soul; find what truly matters; what you believe in. Become your true identity and live your dreams, the way you want to. Connect with others, sharing positive energy where ever you go. Find your purpose. You are you, and you are beautiful.

❖ **I have a toolkit to unlock self-love and self-worth.** With my key in my mind I can unlock my tool box, the kit to my life. This gives me the freedom of self-awareness, to accept others and take action for my thoughts, feelings and behaviour. To love myself unconditionally and to be kind to myself and others. You have your own key to set yourself free, to love yourself and understand your self-worth. Be kind to yourself and others. Keep your toolbox forever, and with your key, you will have everything you need to bring your dreams to life. You're the key.

Stefano D'Agata

- ❖ **There is a God, but he or she is not what you think.** I believe that the entity we call God consists of our collective existence and understanding. The religions mankind has formed to celebrate this entity are entirely a human construct fashioned around inspired individuals and modified to suit various cultural expectations. The fundamental belief all religions share is that we are part of one entity and our purpose in life is to look after each other and the environment we live in.

- ❖ **If you want a loving relationship with someone, you must work at it.** The act of love is giving of oneself. It is not something that just happens. You must work at it. To build a relationship with a special someone requires commitment and understanding. No two people are totally compatible, and it is sometimes the things that make us incompatible that attract us to another person the most. In any relationship therefore, one must be prepared to compromise, to give of oneself and to let others give to you.

- ❖ **Show me the boy at 7 and I will show you the man.** Through writing my chapter in this book, I have discovered that there are character traits and core beliefs which we develop at an early age that we carry throughout our lives.

There are certainly some elements of the man I am now in my 7-year-old self and the spiritual beliefs I developed as a 14-year-old have stayed with me all my life. So, it seems that we are born with an intrinsic nature that governs our personalities and values. But it is how we are nurtured, our interactions with others and our search for knowledge and understanding that cements our personalities and values.

Christine Carmuciano

- ❖ **Talk to yourself with love and forgiveness.** Let your vulnerability soften your heart so that you can let the people around you love you. Don't always believe your own story. You will find that if you tell it to yourself enough times, it will become you and define you! The lines between your story and reality will become blurred, stopping you from recognising the truth along the way. Keep lines of communication open, let people in and if you're not feeling ok, don't be afraid to tell someone for fear of weakness or judgement. It's ok!

- ❖ **There is no need to prove yourself, you are worthy and you are good enough just as you are.** Remember, the people who don't like you as you are, are not your people! Trust your inner voice; it is the one true voice you can count on, for it is only when you stop listening, that you lose yourself. You will find that trying to 'fit in', is not always for your greatest good. Be true to your authentic self and happiness will follow, and the right people will surround you.

❖ **Be conscious of your thoughts and mindset and the words you speak.** Know that you alone have the power within at all times to change your mindset and let your story go. To quote my mother's words again; 'Rosso di Sera, bel tempo si spera!' when the night sky is red, beautiful weather is hoped for. The opposite being; 'Grigio di sera, la pioggia si avvicina!' when the night sky is grey, rain will be approaching.

When we think about our thoughts, they in a way mirror that saying. If we think positive thoughts, (red at night) our vibration is high, therefore settting ourselves up for a good day. We will be in the right frame of mind to handle any obstacles that might potentially taint our day because our attitude is a positive one.

The flip side to that is if we think negative, dark thoughts, (the grey at night), our vibration is low and our attitude a negative one; no matter what crosses our path, we will think it is the end of the world because our mindset is already in a dark place. Hence our day will most probably not be a good one. To quote the words of a dear friend of mine, Antoinette Pellegrini, 'Your Thoughts Matter.'

Diane Psaila

❖ **Creating an environment of nourishment for the mind, body and soul** stems from embracing a belief in yourself and opening up to the possibility of taking the steps in making ambitions a reality. It is important to resist deep-seated fears and inhibitions stemming from bad experiences or fear of failure to surface and act as barriers to living to your full potential.

If you encounter a similar set of circumstances, it does not imply the same outcome. Each challenge is a unique experience and ultimately, how you respond can make all the difference to the result. Taking control can lead to empowerment and promotion of a positive state of mind to face the day to day responsibilities; a will to work at being your best and a coping mechanism when faced with difficulties.

❖ **Wisdom is a gift** that comes with having experienced all that has come before, but it is also an inbred warning system; an instinctive feeling of when something is right or wrong. I have found that with some people there is an instant connection of best intentions at heart like a two-way antidote of nurturing goodness spreading warmth to all in its path.

Acknowledge too, that sometimes it is necessary to shield yourself from those who relish in belittling your worth. It is important to recognise that this is more about their personal insecurities or agendas; therefore it may be best to sever ties with unhealthy relationships as a key to survival. Of course, the choice to remove yourself from a toxic situation is not always possible, however, how you react in situations is completely yours to control and so this is a powerful tool to ensure your self-esteem will remain intact.

❖ **Our personal strengths and weaknesses are our right as unique individuals** therefore we are entitled to explore our strengths that will undoubtedly far outweigh any feelings of inadequacies.

Looking back to our past and reflecting on the experiences that have left an imprint in our minds tells us of the emotional significance of that time; happy, sad, fear, loss, failure and success. They are there, however at the same time, the messages take on a different perspective, a deeper understanding of what was and the surrounding circumstances.

The lessons of yesteryear are all parts of me. An invitation to seek reasoning by sending messages to my younger self to define and settle the grey gaps in my story. Feelings of self-doubt are pushed away to make way to embrace strength and deal with challenges; to persist in following a path of discovery and growth.

Gail Conley

- **Our perspectives on life have been shaped by our experiences.** I have gained my own knowledge and perspectives from the things I witnessed, the good and the bad. I feel that people are generally good and that maybe it is what they have faced throughout their lives that have altered their perceptions. It is through my own experiences, the experiences of my family, friends and acquaintances and the resilience they have shown that has inspired and shaped who I am today.

- **Love, faith, hope and having patience are your best allies.** Love requires you to have faith and hope. Patience allows you to see the broader perspectives as situations and circumstances unfold. I have always told myself that things will be ok. I believe in this wholeheartedly even when faced with life's challenges.

    People can be unpleasant, or things go wrong, but we need to have love, faith, hope and patience and eventually things all come together. If not, this is a lesson in life going forward.

- **Pay it forward - good karma comes to those who do good deeds throughout their life.** Throughout my life, I have tried to be kind, considerate and accommodating to all I come into contact with. If I see a way of helping those in need, I feel it is my purpose to help. I feel gratitude to those who have helped me and in response, I try to return the favour. It costs nothing to smile, and a smile can be contagious. Your smile may be the only love a person gets that day. So smile and be kind. The Angels will hold space for you as one of their divine creatures of the light and pay it forward to you too.

Suzanne Therese Costello

- ❖ **Be prepared to admit that you don't know everything.** Take time to research all the options and look into how to make the changes to your situation that won't disadvantage you later in life. For example, before you leave school, explore all the course options with an adult who has more life experiences than you do.

  Remember how when you left primary school you thought you were so grown up until the first day you walked inside the gates of your huge secondary school with hundreds of students. That feeling is going to happen again and again in your life, whenever you start anything new, but that is part of the learning experience.

I regret that I didn't obtain a qualification. I was able to have a happy life regardless, but that lingering regret remains. Always consider the consequences of your choices, take the advice of others, and choose what will make you happy long term.

❖ **Don't make a big decision based solely on the money that you think you are going to miss out on in the short term**. A temporary sacrifice might make an enormous difference to your earning potential for the rest of your working life. Be prepared to go without some outings and luxuries that in fifty years when you look back will seem such a waste of time and money. Create a life of security for yourself as you are the most important person in your life, and you cannot depend on other people to prop you up, especially as life throws you some curveballs.

❖ **Be open to all sorts of career options**. The right career for you might not even exist when you leave school and start university or college. Technology is moving at such a fast pace that new opportunities are being created every day. The qualification that you first set out to achieve might just become the springboard into a career that satisfies all your needs and rewards you handsomely. This is true at any stage in life. Always to be open to embracing change and opportunities.

Lisa Jane

- ❖ **In solitude, you will hear the answers.** When I was in a state of being alone, I allowed myself to reflect, connect with my soul and listen to my intuition. When life brought challenges, I took time out to lower the volume in my environment and I created a quiet space where I would go beyond my thoughts. When you come out from solitude, you have a clearer perception of self, a knowingness of the path and the action to take is more effective.

- ❖ **With gratitude, you will evolve.** In a moment of lack, saying thank you is powerful. I could've been in a rut my whole life, withholding my truth and falling further and further. Instead, I learnt to look at my challenges as opportunities. With each drawback, I acknowledged the benefits and linked them to my core values. Each time I saw the blessing, my heart opened, and I not only thanked the moment, I also thanked who was involved and myself. To truly experience gratitude, one must let go of judgement to evolve.

- ❖ **Love all your parts unconditionally;** the good, the bad, the ugly and the fabulous. It took time and personal development to truly love myself without conditions. To be ok with what I have done to myself, to others and what has been done to me. I do not have any regrets.

I wouldn't go back and change a thing. Every part of our being serves a purpose.

Kathy Zisiadis

- ❖ **Being unique and different is awesome.** I have now embraced the strength in my left hand. The sooner you accept and recognise your special qualities, whatever they may be, the sooner you appreciate that your individuality is magnificent. There will only ever be one of you.

- ❖ **Your experiences make you a stronger person.** Although daunting at the time, experiencing and surviving the trauma and difficulties in your life makes you a more brave, resilient and stronger human being. Don't be so hard on yourself. Trauma is not your fault. Give yourself permission to cry and heal. Stop blaming yourself, you did what you could, and that was enough.

- ❖ **Be grateful and have faith in your journey.** Don't regret the past. Everything happens for a reason; it prepares you for where you're going next.

Anne-Marie Donis

- **Surrender the pain that feeling guilty gives you and replace it with feeling loved.** Guilt is a perception that our mind creates when other people blame you for something that is not necessarily your fault. Guilt is only real if you allow it to be.

- **Believe in yourself and master your own destiny.** Life will always have adversities, but that doesn't mean you can't overcome them. We all have an inner strength that we can rely on to help us when we need it most.

- **Be kind to yourself and see the good in all you are.** You are unique and have so much to offer the world. Nothing is impossible, and when you find that confidence to stand up for yourself, you will be unstoppable.

Author Bios

Christine Carmuciano

Christine Carmuciano is in her mid-fifties, a single mother of two, now young adults, Adrian and Stephanie.

Mother-in-law to Lara and Will and a very proud grandmother to her precious little grandson, Xavier and a new one on the way, still to make his appearance into this world.

At 55 and having worked in the banking industry for most of her adult life, she became one of the numbers in a harsh restructure. She found herself at a juxtaposition. Although she was grateful to the industry for giving her the stability and security she needed as a young single mum and the skills to move up through the ranks in the industry, she knew it no longer aligned with who she was.

She decided to close that chapter on her life and embark on a new one she knew nothing about. All she knew was that she wanted to explore her creative side, give back to society in some way and live a more fulfilling life, rather than continue to destroy her soul in an environment she no longer identified with.

With these thoughts and her new mantra, 'I find true success through inner fulfilment' (by Deepak Chopra); she set out to explore her options. She has recently completed a Cert III in Education Support and is currently studying for a Diploma in Art Therapy. She still has no idea what her ultimate path will look like, but she is excited to find out and happy to be on the journey of self-discovery.

Her spiritual side is also very important to her; she has a passion for the healing modalities of Reiki and Pellowah, amongst others. Her hunger to learn more is never satisfied. She is in her element when she is open to the Universe and self-development. Her happy place is being in nature, the peaceful sound of a river nearby with the sun's rays glistening like crystals on the water. This is where she is reminded of gratitude for everything she has experienced in life and everything she now has in her life.

The very raw and honest lessons in her chapter are written as not only an awakening and awareness for herself and others, but especially for her children, who endured more than what they should have, but who are now wiser than their years because of it.

Gail Conley

Gail Conley grew up in the northern suburbs of Melbourne in Glenroy.

She is a 52-year-old woman who has experienced childhood domestic violence, death and trauma throughout her life.

She has cared for mentally ill family members and has opened her home to both family and friends needing a hand. Her purpose has always been to help people find their way, and she is grateful to those who have helped her find hers.

Gail met her soulmate and the love of her life in 1981. She lived with her husband Brett and two boys in Craigieburn for the past 23 years until November 2018 when she moved with her husband to a 114-acre farm on the beautiful Lake Victoria in Gippsland. A new life and a sea change in the country. There they are farming sheep and cattle and Gail is running her business *Chakra Angel Oracle* from her new home, which she describes as 'Paradise'. It is a sanctuary for creatures great and small, a place of love, peace and harmony for all. She thanks the universe for providing her with this vision and delivering this wonderful place.

She was working in the Community Health sector as a Senior Administration/Payroll Officer for 29 years until end February 2015. It was then that she answered the call that she had been manifesting for many years, and realising her dream, she began *Chakra Angel Oracle*.

Her spiritually based business provides a place where her clients can request an authentic and true reading or healing. She uses creativity to bring her focus and balance and loves to create and sell handcrafted and personally sourced spiritual products.

Writing for this book, *A Message to Your Younger Self*, Book 2 of the, *We Inspire Now Series*, is an opportunity to tell some of her life stories in the hope of helping others and of healing herself.

To see more about Gail Conley go to www.chakraangeloracle.com

Suzanne Therese Costello

Suzanne Therese Costello has always enjoyed writing, whether it is her annual Christmas Epistle or long letters to her many friends and family across the globe.

She corresponds with hundreds of friends via email and her favourite social media platform, Facebook.

Suzanne worked in many varied positions from clerical to sales and customer service over the years while she raised her three children with her husband Ian in the eastern suburbs of Melbourne.

She is now happily retired and enjoying time with their adult children and four beautiful grandchildren. Suzanne is an outgoing person who grew up in country Victoria attending several secondary schools when her father's job took them to another town. She attributes her friendliness to that country upbringing and always likes to see the best in everyone and every challenge that life has thrown her.

Her health issues have given her opportunities to put into practice the tools she has learned over the years at a range of self-development courses. She credits mindfulness training with reducing her stress levels over the past nine years.

She has written an unpublished memoir and several short stories. In 2011 The Ballan Historical Society published three of her stories in its July newsletter.

She is currently writing a series of short stories after attending writing workshops.

Stefano D'Agata

Stefano, AKA Steve, AKA Stephen, AKA Stevie D, is a man of many names and many facets. A Civil Engineer, specialising in asset management and infrastructure planning in water services and local government sectors, he has also found time to follow artistic pursuits.

Born to parents who migrated to Australia in the 1950s, Steve is the 5th of 7 children, and his ethnic background covers six countries over four continents. In the 1990s, Steve met and married his wife Maria and went on to produce a family of three children. Sadly, less than 20 years after they first met, Maria lost a six-year-long battle with breast cancer, and Steve has been a single parent ever since.

In mid-life, Steve has sought to re-connect with his artistic side and has written an (unpublished) satirical novel on the papacy, collaborated on the first instalments of the *We Inspire Now* anthology series, started a YouTube cooking show and has presented his written work and performed stand-up comedy at various open mic venues.

Steve lives in Melbourne, Australia with his three frustratingly fabulous children and various pets.

Anne Marie Donis

Anne-Marie Donis is a 61-year-old woman who has lived a life of many challenges and adversities. She has three wonderful children who she loves and four beautiful grandsons she dotes on. Family is one of the most important things in Anne-Marie's life.

Throughout her long-spanning career of various jobs, Anne-Marie was always looking to find that inner peace and contentment that most people seek throughout life.

Even though she suffered major health issues throughout her life, including being close to death, Anne-Marie overcame all her obstacles to move forward for a much better life.

As a mature age student, Anne-Marie made the big sacrifice to go back to College, while raising her children and taking care of the family. At the age of 32, Anne-Marie's dream of becoming a teacher came true. This was the start of a wonderful new chapter in Anne-Marie's life which included running her own successful Holistic Centre.

Then Anne-Marie's life took a major turn for the worse. Her marriage had failed despite many attempts at reconciliation. This never stopped Anne-Marie from moving forward. It made her stronger and more determined to find her true self.

Anne-Marie has learnt through her friends and family who always supported her, that it is okay to be her true self. Something she had never done before.

This has enabled Anne-Marie to take the next exciting journey in her life and become an author. She contributed to the first book in the *We Inspire Now Series*, called *Live Your Truth* and hopes that this is just the beginning of a new career for her.

Finally, Anne-Marie has found that inner peace she was looking for and continues to help others to do the same.

Lisa Jane Hussey

Based in the northern area of Melbourne, Australia, Lisa Jane is an aspiring humanitarian with a magnetic smile and charismatic nature. She educates and entertains with her stories bringing balance to life experiences.

Lisa Jane is skilful in getting to the core of a problem and treats the cause not just the symptoms to health and well-being.

With her educational background in Behavioural Sciences and Beauty & Skin Therapy, she has bridged the gap by offering a way to let go, heal and move forward consciously. A passion for Holistic Living, Lisa Jane brings the study of Ayurveda and Traditional Chinese Medicine into her practices.

Lisa Jane is certified in the Process of Equilibration®, the Wealth Principles® and the Chi Cycle Lifestyle®. These modalities guide people to live life inspired and in harmony.

Lisa Jane's purpose is to show people a way to free themselves of the conditions that have been placed and for them to create their own unique path.

www.lisajanehussey.com

Lisa Locks

Lisa Locks is a mother of two beautiful adult children and mother to their partners and their dogs. Lisa also shares her house with many international students of different nationalities and borders and runs her own hairdressing business from home. There is never a dull moment in her house since there are a lot of people coming in and out every day.

Lisa has always been in tune with her children and others. The realisation of how much love she has for children has inspired her to write children's books. Lisa understands that every child is different and therefore believes that it is important to provide good, fundamental guidelines, and for each child to know that loving themselves is the key. Once they know that, everything else falls into place.

Through the years of hardship of being divorced, raising her two children, dealing with the constant juggling act of work, school-runs and sports activities that has kept her busy, Lisa has been able to grow as a person and gradually come to understand how to love herself with all her flaws. She has learnt to love and accept herself and become aware and take responsibility for her own decisions. Lisa's positive attitude and her own belief system, which she calls her 'key', underpins her ongoing motivation and commitment and allows her to reach for her dreams and goals.

Lisa's determination, even her little feistiness and frustrations, keeps her passion alive which allows her to love and enjoy every minute that she lives .Lisa aims to 'Live in my thoughts, my feelings and my behaviour - my words are my world.' With this powerful message, Lisa aspires to spread a positive energy wherever she goes, thereby shaping the future generations.

Her motto is: *Being kind is always on my mind.*

www.lisalockshairdressingsalon.com

Antoinette Pellegrini

Antoinette Pellegrini lives in a leafy Melbourne suburb in Victoria, Australia.

She is an Author, Teacher, Writing Coach and a Personal Development and Mindfulness Consultant.

She raised two amazing young men as a single mother and overcame many hardships and challenges throughout her life.

This anthology, *A Message to Your Younger Self: What Would You Say?*, is the second book in Antoinette's anthology series called *We Inspire Now* . Antoinette created this anthology series in the hope of inspiring people to look within themselves, heal past hurts, and have the courage to pursue and achieve their goals.

The first book in the anthology series, *Live Your Truth* (2018), featured regular people who were daring to follow their dreams and help inspire others to do the same.

Antoinette's first book published in 2017, *Your Thoughts Matter: The Future You Are Creating Starts Now* and the accompanying *Reflection Journal* and *Affirmation Cards,* contain 25 Reflections and Affirmations on connection and the power of positive thinking and conscious choice. It is designed to empower and inspire the reader to create the life they would like to live.

Antoinette is also a secondary school teacher, working as a teacher for several years before starting a corporate career. Antoinette left the corporate world in 2016 to follow her passion in writing and helping others find their voice and achieve their personal goals.

Antoinette has helped people achieve their personal aspirations, improve their wellbeing, energy levels and happiness. As a writing coach she has enabled people to make their dreams of being published authors a reality. Her focus is on the link between mind, body and spirit and the critical part the mind plays in relation to overall health, wellbeing and achievement of goals.

Antoinette offers one on one consultations, motivational coaching, personal development and writing workshops and courses.

www.antoinettepellegrini.com

www.weinspirenowbooks.com

Diane Psaila

Diane Psaila lives in the north-east fringe of Melbourne in a setting of leafy, undulating hills amidst the seasonal beauty and sounds of nature.

Customer relations and administration have been her primary areas of employment, the last thirteen years at secondary colleges, undertaking a diversity of tasks in a busy and vibrant environment. In recent years Diane has proudly delved into realising her ambition in having her creative writings published in various forums including contributing as one of the co-authors in the *We Inspire Now Series,* Book 1*: Live Your Truth, 2018* and Book 2*: A Message To Your Younger Self: What Would You Say? 2020.*

Blessed to be a devoted mother and grandmother, Diane recalls her youth, a realm of special family memories and an era of traditional values that demanded adherence, therefore shaping her impressionable young mind. Growth brought on the concept of a deviation from the norm. This attributed to her experiencing episodes of tough times, and when confronted with a mentality of a resolute black or white, finding the courage to venture into a grey often meant there was a consequence.

Looking back to her past from a point of hindsight and wisdom has been the inspiration in contributing as a co-author to these insightful books. Painting a picture in the reader's mind, Diane recalls pivotal points in her life, the valuable lessons and the awareness of underlying feelings that connect associations with behaviours. Personal growth involves the realisation that everyone and everything we come into contact with teaches you something.

The messages are nourishment for the soul, like enveloping a good deed, misgiving or hurt with a newfound energy to enhance, protect and urge a fulfilling way forward. This adds a greater dimension to the thinking process in reinforcing the concept that self-worth is heightened by living authentically.

Diane is embracing opportunities, walking proudly forward, nurturing the unique gift that is her life and encourages others to do the same.

Challenges are only obstacles in life's journey that make the determination to see a desired result an even greater feeling of success. Diane Psaila April 2019

I dedicate my writings to precious family. You are my love and my pride. I wish to acknowledge too, treasured friends, who each in their unique way have influenced and journeyed with me the tide of life's mishaps and successes. Diane Psaila

Kathy Zisiadis

Kathy Zisiadis was born and raised in inner Melbourne, Australia and is a postgraduate from the University of Melbourne. She is an Author, Teacher and Designer.

Her extensive experience includes corporate training and teaching secondary school students.

Over the years she developed and cultivated her writing not only through teaching but also through writing about life experiences and sharing them with the wider community.

She has written numerous articles and has contributed both to English and Greek newspapers, namely Neos Kosmos. She has also worked as an interpreter and translator on various articles, poems and song lyrics. She is excited to be a contributing author in the *We Inspire Now* book series.

In *Live Your Truth,* the first book of the *We Inspire Now Series*, she was inspired to write about her passion for landscape architectural design which stems from her life's journey; her love and enthusiasm for gardens became more apparent and developed in the aftermath of the breakdown of her marriage; she found herself more drawn to the natural environment, which offered her a sense of healing, a sense of peace and tranquility.

The hardships and difficulties she's endured as a single mum have been blessings in disguise. They helped her to build character, strength, courage, determination and willpower, and inspired her to share her story with others; to seek happiness and ultimately to live her truth.

In the second book, *A Message to Your Younger Self: What Would You Say?*, we get a glimpse into her early life. We get an insight of the traumatic incidences she encountered as a child. We discover her experiences of the Australian public school system, the drawbacks of being the firstborn child to immigrant parents and the consequences of being 'left handed' during the late 1970's.

Writing for the second book has been a reflective journey into her childhood, and somewhat healing. Her work and this story is proudly dedicated to her beloved parents Bill and Joanna, whom as immigrants sacrificed and worked very hard to provide her with the best life tools and valuable childhood memories.

Books Previously Published by the Authors in this Anthology

Live Your Truth

Book 1 *We Inspire Now Series*

Authors: Antoinette Pellegrini, Stefano D'Agata, Anne-Marie Donis, Diane Psaila and Kathy Zisiadis (2018)

Ten authors share their stories about overcoming hardships and difficulties to pursue their goals, discover who they are and live their own truth.

Available at all major online retailers and at
www.antoinettepellegrini.com

Your Thoughts Matter: The Future You Are Creating Starts Now

By Antoinette Pellegrini (2017)

Reflections and Affirmations on connection and the power of positive thinking and conscious choice.

It is designed to inspire the reader to create the life they would love to live.

Available at all major online retailers and at:

www.antoinettepellegrini.com

Accompaniments to the *Your Thoughts Matter* book

By Antoinette Pellegrini (2017)

Your Thoughts Matter Reflection Journal

Your Thoughts Matter Affirmation Cards

Available at:
www.antoinettepellegrini.com

www.ingramcontent.com/pod-product-compliance
Lightning Source LLC
Chambersburg PA
CBHW070729020526
44107CB00077B/2158